Fokker Dr I Aces of World War 1

SERIES EDITOR: TONY HOLMES

OSPREY AIRCRAFT OF THE ACES • 40

Fokker Dr I Aces of World War 1

Norman Franks and Greg VanWyngarden

OSPREY
AVIATION

Front cover
20 April 1918 – Rittmeister Manfred Freiherr von Richthofen, commander of *Jagdgeschwader Nr I*, achieves his 79th and 80th victories to become the 'ace of aces' of all nations in World War 1.

Led by Richthofen in his scarlet Fokker Dr I 425/17, seven Triplanes of *Jagdstaffel* 11 engaged a patrol of Sopwith Camels from No 3 Sqn of the newly-formed RAF east of Villers-Brettoneaux. Seeing a Fokker being attacked by one of the British fighters, the Rittmeister fastened on to the tail of the Camel, flown by Maj Richard Raymond-Barker. After only a few accurate shots from Richthofen's guns, the Camel (D6439) exploded in flames and Raymond-Barker was killed.

With scarcely a pause, Richthofen was soon firing at Camel B7393, flown by 19-year-old Rhodesian 2Lt David G Lewis. The fighter's fuel tanks were soon hit and set on fire, but Lewis managed to cut his engine and dive to the ground, being thrown clear from the crash. Dazed, scorched, but alive, Lewis staggered to his feet and saw the blazing wreckage of Raymond-Barker's machine only 50 yards away. Richthofen soared overhead at low level and waved at German infantry who were coming to take Lewis prisoner.

The very next day, the *Jagdgeschwader* commander would meet his own fate and come down behind British lines in 425/17, forever linking the 'Red Baron' with the Fokker Triplane in history, and the popular imagination (*cover artwork by Iain Wyllie*)

Back cover
Pour le Mérite winner Ltn Hans Kirschstein was *Jasta* 6's 'ace of aces', claiming 27 kills up until his death in a flying accident on 16 July 1918

Title page spread
Jasta 14's Fokker Dr I 389/17 (Werk-Nr 2115) was nicknamed *Maria*, and it is seen between patrols at Phalempin airfield in early June 1918. The fighter's unit marking took the form of the lengthwise black and white stripe that bisected the fuselage. The background colour to the *Maria* titling is unknown, as are the identities of the two pilots admiring the Triplane

First published in Great Britain in 2001 by Osprey Publishing, Elms Court, Chapel Way, Botley, Oxford, OX2 9LP
E-mail: info@ospreypublishing.com

ISBN 1 84176 223 7

Edited by Tony Holmes
Page design by TT Designs, T & B Truscott
Cover Artwork by Iain Wyllie
Aircraft Profiles by Harry Dempsey
Scale Drawings by Mark Styling
Index by Alan Thatcher
Origination by Grasmere Digital Imaging, Leeds, UK
Printed through Bookbuilders, Hong Kong

01 02 03 04 05   10 9 8 7 6 5 4 3 2 1

EDITOR'S NOTE
To make this best-selling series as authoritative as possible, the Editor would be interested in hearing from any individual who may have relevant photographs, documentation or first-hand experiences relating to the elite fighter pilots, and their aircraft, of the various theatres of war. Any material used will be credited to its original source. Please write to Tony Holmes at 10 Prospect Road, Sevenoaks, Kent, TN13 3UA, Great Britain, or by e-mail at: tony.holmes@osprey-jets.freeserve.co.uk

ACKNOWLEDGEMENTS
The authors wish to thank Peter M Grosz, Peter Kilduff, George H Williams, H H Wynne, Stephen Lawson, Ray Rimell, Frau Margot Hemer, D S Abbott, Rick Duiven, Paul S Leaman, Neal O'Connor and many others who supplied photographs and information which helped in the compilation of this work. The many books of Peter Kilduff were also of great use, as were those by Alex Imrie (especially his superb work *The Fokker Triplane*), which provided much valuable data. Finally, both O'Brien Browne and Jan Hayzlett were most generous in supplying their wonderful translations of German material.

For a catalogue of all Osprey Publishing titles please contact us at:

Osprey Direct UK, PO Box 140, Wellingborough, Northants, NN8 4ZA, UK
E-mail: info@ospreydirect.co.uk

Osprey Direct USA, c/o Motorbooks International, 729 Prospect Ave, PO Box 1, Osceola, WI 54020, USA
E-mail: info@ospreydirectusa.com

Or visit our website: www.ospreypublishing.com

CONTENTS

DUBIOUS DEBUT

The brilliant Dutch aircraft designer Anthony Fokker had first gained international fame with the success of his series of *Eindecker* (monoplane) fighters, armed with the new synchronised machine gun firing through the airscrew arc, in 1915. The Fokker E-series of fighters had ruled the air until early 1916, yet in the skies over the Battle of Verdun in the spring and summer they were outflown by the nimble French Nieuport 11 sesquiplanes (see *Osprey Aircraft of the Aces 33 - Nieuport Aces of World War 1* for further details).

The end of the Fokker monoplane's dominance became truly evident during the Battle of the Somme in July, when the *Eindeckers* were driven from the air by more manoeuvrable British biplane fighters like the 'pusher' configuration DH 2 and FE 8. Anthony Fokker's star was waning, and he would not regain his reputation as the supplier of the best German fighter aircraft for some time.

Experienced German fighter pilots like Oswald Boelcke and Rudolf Berthold had seen the writing on the wall for some time, and had asked for the development of light biplane fighters, but the *Fliegertruppe* (Aviation Troops) command and *Idflieg* (The Inspectorate of Aviation Troops) had been slow to respond. However, in March 1916 *Idflieg* placed its first order for biplane fighters with the Halberstadt firm, purchasing 12 of its D I type. Fokker followed with his D I, powered by the 120 hp in-line Mercedes D II engine and armed with a single machine gun. This machine was not a success, and was withdrawn from the Front because of fatal wing failures caused by deficient and negligent workmanship.

The succeeding Fokker D II and D III biplanes, powered by rotary Oberursel engines, were somewhat more successful, but still found deficient in comparison with the powerful and strongly constructed Albatros D I and D II fighters (see *Osprey Aircraft of the Aces 32 - Albatros Aces of World War 1* for further details). The Albatros firm would retain the lion's share of the single-seat fighter business with the advent of their D III (its sesquiplane layout inspired by the Nieuport), and its successor the D V and D Va, throughout the remainder of 1917. Albatros fighters would form the main equipment of the *Jagdstaffeln* (literally 'hunting section', or fighter squadron, abbreviated as *Jasta*) until mid-1918.

The Royal Naval Air Service's introduction of a three-winged fighter (the Sopwith Triplane) in February 1917 made a deep impression on German pilots and, subsequently, the German aircraft industry. Not that three-winged aircraft were new – designers had worked on triplanes since before the war, but the Sopwith fighter was the first to be built in quantity. Generally, three-winged aeroplanes were rarely favoured, but the Sopwith's light, yet powerful engine (the 110 hp Clerget 9Z, replaced by the 130 hp Clerget 9b in the summer) helped its success.

In the hands of a good pilot, the Sopwith was superior to the Albatros fighters then in service. Rittmeister Manfred von Richthofen encountered the new triplane in combat in April 1917, and later wrote, '. . . the Sopwith Triplane is the best aircraft the enemy possesses. It climbs better, is more manoeuvrable, and does not lose altitude in a bank, is faster and can be dived straight down'. Richthofen's friend, and fellow *Jasta* 11 ace Kurt Wolff concurred that the Sopwith was superior to the D III in speed, manoeuvrability and rate of climb.

So, before long *Idflieg* underwrote a huge programme for the development of three-winged prototype designs. Fokker was already working on the concept for a fighter with three wings, the design's origin going back to early 1917, when Anthony Fokker and his team began construction of two experimental biplanes powered by a 160 hp Mercedes engine. A third, roughly contemporary, biplane (company designation D VI) was powered by the Oberursel Ur II rotary, which was a copy of the French 110 hp Le Rhône.

This aircraft had been built as a demonstration machine for Austria-Hungary. However, in mid-stream, the D VI biplane was altered to a triplane configuration (later Fokker designation V4, Works number 1661). And by 5 July 1917, Fokker's fourth prototype had been ordered as a triplane. This aircraft was also designated D VI (later V5, Works number 1697) and it is this machine which became the true Dr I prototype.

The Fokker design was entirely original, and no mere copy of the Sopwith, the Dutch designer using a cantilever wing structure that he had previously worked on in his revolutionary sesquiplane designs (V1 through V3). The wings were built around two box spars coupled together, and ailerons were fitted only to the upper wing, eventually modified into aerodynamically balanced (extended) ailerons. The lower two wings were of basically equal chord, although each was of slightly shorter span than the wing just above it.

The three wings were supported by what looked like one interplane strut each side, but each strut was in two pieces – not one large strut passing through from upper to lower wing. These struts were supports for the cantilever design, and were added to increase wing rigidity.

The final type V4 passed all tests and was put into production, and the order was made on 14 July 1917 for 20 machines (including the four prototype V4 aircraft, the last three of which were given the designation of F I and numbered 101/17, 102/17 and 103/17). Later, the designation would change to Dr I ('Dr' standing for *Dreidecker*, or triplane), and further orders would bring the total produced to 320. Armament consisted of two synchronised Maxim LMG 08/15 'Spandau' machine guns fitted in front of the cockpit, and set to fire through the propeller arc.

Aircraft F I 101/17 was tested to destruction (this occurred on 11 August 1917), whilst the remaining two machines (F I 102 and 103/17) were sent to France for frontline evaluation. They were carried by railway to *Armee-Flug-Park* 4 (*AFP* 4, or Army Aircraft Replacement Park 4), for allocation to Rittmeister Manfred von Richthofen's *Jagdgeschwader Nr I*, near Courtrai.

Rittmeister Manfred Baron von Richthofen (far right), commander of JG I, poses with Konstantin Krefft, Anthony Fokker (also wearing a flying helmet) and Kurt Wolff (*via Franks collection*)

JG I was Germany's first fighter 'wing' which was composed of four *Jagdstaffeln* permanently grouped together – *Jastas* 4, 6, 10 and 11. By this time, of course, von Richthofen was the leading German fighter ace and the first *Geschwader* leader, so it was logical that he and his men, including his very competent technical officer Ltn Konstantin Krefft, should test the new machine.

Anthony Fokker knew von Richthofen well, for the Rittmeister had visited his factory at Schwerin, and consistently tried to stay informed of the latest aeronautical advances made by Fokker, and other significant manufacturers (as early as 25 July, he had told his men, 'You will receive new Fokker triplanes, which climb like apes and are as manoeuvrable as the devil').

Fokker F I 102/17 was used by Baron von Richthofen to gain his 61st victory, and was later flown by Kurt Wolff on his last flight. The F I machines did not have the wingtip skids seen on production Dr I aircraft. The cowling and wheel covers of 102/17 were a dark, solid, colour which was probably olive-brown, although red may have been applied to these components at a later date (*via VanWyngarden*)

For his part, Anthony Fokker had always consciously and cleverly maintained a good relationship with the leading aces. He listened to their needs and desires, and showered them with gifts and lavish parties – he was, after all, no older than many of them – and was never shy about cultivating publicity in the limelight accorded to Germany's great aces.

It appears that great things were expected of the new Fokker triplane as the first two examples were delivered in late August – these aircraft would be flown in combat by three of the most successful and celebrated of the current fighter pilots: Richthofen, *Jasta* 11 commander Oblt Kurt Wolff and the mercurial and aggressive Ltn Werner Voss, *Staffelführer* of *Jasta* 10. The weather was bad so it was not until the evening of the 28th that Voss was able to make a test flight in 103/17, and probably von Richthofen flew 102/17 at the same time.

On 31 August Tony Fokker, his motion picture camera (he was a dedicated ciné-photographer) and the PR men were in evidence at the *Jasta* 11 field at Marckebeeke, along with Gen Sixt von Arnim, Chief of the 4th Army, General Staff Maj-Gen von Lossberg and the German Chancellor Georg Michaelis, all of whom had come to see the new triplane. Anthony Fokker himself was photographed in the cockpit of 102/17, and there is

On 31 August 1917, Anthony Fokker demonstrated his new F I 102/17 to a collection of dignitaries at *Jasta* 11's airfield at Marckebeeke. Here, Fokker is seen in the cockpit as Maj-Gen von Lossberg rests his arm on the fuselage next to Manfred von Richthofen, leader of JG I. Next is Karl Bodenschatz, JG I's adjutant, and Ltn Hans Adam of *Jasta* 6. This view clearly shows the curved leading edge of the tailplane, which was one of the distinguishing characteristics of the pre-production F I machines. These F Is were probably finished in an overall coat of undersurface light blue – over this the Fokker camouflage of a greyish olive-brown was applied, resulting in a typical streaky finish to the uppersurfaces (*via Van Wyngarden*)

little doubt that he took the opportunity to fly and demonstrate the new fighter to the dignitaries, as well as to the pilots of JG I.

Following the demonstration, and all the hype with the top brass, the Richthofen *Geschwader* was left with the two new triplanes. Richthofen, himself, still had his head bandaged from the wound he had received on 6 July in a fight with FE 2s of No 20 Sqn. He had been lucky to survive, and despite his 57 victories, and exceptional experience, he was something of a changed man since that near-death encounter. He suffered from constant headaches which were worsened by flying, and was left exhausted after every mission.

After a period in hospital and some leave, von Richthofen had returned to his command in mid-August, and in what is thought to have been his first operational flight since then, he shot down opponent number 58 on 16 August, flying his red Albatros D V 2059/17 – number 59 came ten days later. With only a few exceptions whilst flying the Halberstadt D II, his victories had all been achieved flying the Albatros D II, D III or D V.

There can be little doubt that von Richthofen was a major influence on getting the triplane to the Front, and therefore it was logical that this distinguished airman and fighter ace would be among the first to make use of it. However, the rotary engine was not favoured by many pilots, and the Fokker triplane, while very manoeuvrable, was fated to be slow. In any case, von Richthofen liked to dogfight and to get in close, and he could do this with a triplane, especially if his fighter opponents would stay and try to dogfight him. The Rittmeister was a capable pilot, but not a natural one. He did not take any joy in flying, but did so out of a sense of duty – he even forbade his pilots to perform aerobatics.

When Oblt Peter Lampel (an ex-bomber pilot turned journalist) asked him in April 1918, 'Is there no more passion in flying?', von Richthofen replied, 'No! Absolutely not! I would much rather be a cavalryman than a flier. Much more. There is nothing special in flying for me. I also have never looped – never! I also forbid my gentlemen to do this, and am utterly uncompromising on this . . . we don't need aerial acrobats, rather go-getters! My gentlemen know this exactly, too . . . I am only excited by air combat, that prickling in the nerves when everything gets going and when I get into a shoot-out with someone. I always hang tight on his tail, dive down on him and then pull up. I never shoot at the machine – I always shoot straight at the pilot. When an observer is also there, the observer is of course the first so that I can avoid his machine gun fire. And yet it is very odd that my last victories were all flamers. But I repeat to you once again – not flying but aerial combat is my main goal in life'.

Like his mentor Oswald Boelcke, von Richthofen's approach to air combat was simple. Get in close and shoot straight – and the triplane was suited for these tactics.

INTO COMBAT

Ask anyone with just a passing interest in the Great War which German aeroplane they think of first, and more than likely they will say the Fokker triplane, and probably in the same breath mention the *Red Baron*. So much has been written about Manfred von Richthofen that this is not surprising. In light of its fame, however, what is surprising is that the Fokker triplane was only at the Front for a relatively short period.

Rittmeister Manfred von Richthofen sits on the wheel of a Fokker triplane which appears to be painted in factory finish – except perhaps for a red cowling? Note the manufacturer's plate on the cowling. Dogs were a favourite of many pilots, and here the Baron gazes at his Danish hound 'Moritz' (*via VanWyngarden*)

Whereas the Albatros Scouts, and later in 1918, the Fokker D VII biplanes equipped virtually every German fighter unit, the Dr I was only issued to around 15 *Jastas*, with the odd one or two being on strength with a few others. In all, only 320 triplanes were built, whereas the Albatros biplanes and Fokker D VIIs were built in far greater numbers.

As an example, even though in September 1918 the Fokker D VII was the main fighter type, there were still 327 Albatros D V and D Va machines in frontline service. In May 1918, just as the D VII was arriving, the number of Albatros Scouts in service topped 1000! The heyday of the triplane was relatively short – perhaps from February to June 1918 – and its true impact on the aerial war was not very substantial.

It can be seen therefore, that in comparison, this mere handful of Dr Is has caught the popular imagination. This is due in no small measure to its association with its main exponent, von Richthofen, together with his 'Circus', and a few extraordinary pilots like Voss and Josef Jacobs.

Rittmeister Baron Manfred Siegfried von Richthofen, holder of the *Pour le Mérite*, prepared for his first war patrol in the new triplane on the morning of 1 September – the day after the publicity presentation of 102/17 and 103/17. The fighter was so new that it had not been painted on any part with the red dope that denoted not only the Baron, but his *Jagdstaffel* 11 as well. It had standard streaked olive brown factory finish camouflage over a light greyish-blue finish which resulted in a neutral, greyish general impression. The black national iron cross insignia on the wings and fuselage were on a white background. The rudder was also white, while the undersides were a shade of light greyish-blue.

The Rittmeister took off at 0750 hrs in company with four others in Albatros D V fighters, and near Zonnebeke, inside the German lines, he spotted a British two-seater – a 'very courageously flown' RE 8 from No 6 Sqn. The crew had been airborne an hour, flying an artillery observation sortie near Polygon Wood, east of Ypres.

As von Richthofen approached to attack, it appears obvious that the two British airmen were faced with a bit of a quandary. Heading straight for them was a three-winged aeroplane, and the only such type they knew about was the Sopwith Triplane. Was it being chased by four Albatros Scouts, and was joining the RE 8 for mutual protection? And if they did not see, or positively identify, the other four biplanes, did they for a moment or two think that this naval pilot was playing about? Surely he would not attack them.

Although the Sopwith Camel was starting to replace the Sopwith Triplanes, there were still some about, and only a few miles north it was known that the French Navy had some Sopwith Triplanes too. Whatever went through the minds of the two RFC flyers in those last seconds is not known, for both men died. Hit by von Richthofen's deadly fire, their machine went down in an uncontrolled spin to crash inside German lines. The Rittmeister acknowledged that in all probability he had been mistaken for a naval Sopwith pilot, as he noted that the British observer stood upright without making a move for his machine gun.

It was at this time that some of the most famous motion-picture footage of the 1914-18 aerial war was shot. Tony Fokker was still on hand at the *Jasta* 11 airfield at Marckebeeke, and he filmed 102/17 being wheeled out of its hangar and the mechanics priming the engine. Von Richthofen is

The Baron's 61st victory was this No 46 Sqn Pup, which he downed on 3 September 1917. As it happened, Anthony Fokker was on a visit to Marckebeeke at the time, and he drove to the site with von Richthofen and Ltn Eberhardt Moehnicke (11 victories, far left), where they met Lt A F Bird, who survived his shoot-down, and had photographs and a ciné film taken. Fokker is wearing Bird's flying helmet and coat (*via VanWyngarden*)

seen putting on his flight gear, pulling his leather helmet on over his bandaged head, and climbing into the cockpit and checking his guns, before a quick taxi and take-off. Werner Voss and Fokker were filmed with F I 103/17 at around this time too.

On 3 September the Baron scored victory number 61 – a Sopwith Pup of No 46 Sqn. Its pilot, Lt A F Bird, put up a stiff fight despite his inferior aircraft. Richthofen reported;

'Along with five aeroplanes from *Staffel* 11, while engaged in a fight with a Sopwith single-seater, I attacked, at a height of 3500 metres, one of the enemy machines. After a fairly long dogfight, I forced him to land near Bousbecque. I was absolutely convinced I had a very skilful pilot in front of me, who even at an altitude of 50 metres did not give up, but fired again, and opened fire on a column of troops while flattening out, then deliberately ran his machine into a tree. Fokker triplane F I Nr 102/17 was absolutely superior to the British Sopwith.'

In all fairness, the last statement is hardly surprising, as the Pup had been in service since October 1916, and was now obsolete. Bird came down not far from the German airfield and shortly von Richthofen, some of his pilots, and Anthony Fokker were at the scene, Fokker taking ciné camera shots of the RFC pilot and his victor. Fokker and the Rittmeister were also filmed examining the downed Pup, and Bird was filmed looking somewhat sheepish, and yet relieved to be alive after his encounter with Germany's most accomplished fighter ace.

Strangely enough, the RFC flyers, who were obviously unaware of the new type, initially thought the appearance of a triplane with German markings had more sinister implications, as recorded by No 46 Sqn pilot Arthur Gould Lee upon hearing of the action on 3 September;

'Five of A Flight . . . met Richthofen's Circus and had a hectic scrap. The Pups were completely outclassed by the D Vs, and most of their share of the fighting consisted of trying to avoid being riddled. Mac and Bird were seen to go down in Hunland. Asher might have reached the Lines.

11

The two chaps who got away, badly shot about, said that one of the Huns was flying a triplane, coloured red. It must be a captured naval Tripe, I suppose.'

Lee wrote this in his book *No Parachute*, and must have added the 'red' description later with the benefit of hindsight after he found out it was Richthofen. The colour of F. I 102/17 was not red, though it is slightly possible that at some point its cowling, and perhaps wheel covers, were painted in this colour.

With his score at 61, von Richthofen left the Front on 6 September for home leave, and would not return until 23 October. It is difficult to discover if his 102/17 was flown by other pilots in early September. It would seem obvious that if anybody was going to fly them it would be the *Staffelführers* – Kurt von Döring of *Jasta* 4 (although he was now in temporary command of JG I in the Baron's absence), Hans Adam of *Jasta* 6, or Kurt Wolff, who arrived back from hospital on the 11th. None of these appear to have done so, however.

Voss had returned to Schwerin with Fokker for a few days in order to test-fly the new V5, but the dates of this brief visit are difficult to pin down. He was certainly at the Front on 3, 5 and 6 September, as he achieved victories on those dates.

While Voss scored ten kills during the time that 103/17 was at *Jagdstaffel* 10, incomplete records make it impossible to determine exactly how many of those victories were achieved in the triplane. The only official record discovered thus far is an Austrian war archive document dated 25 October 1917, which reports that Voss obtained three victories in the triplane. The true total certainly may have been a few more than that, but not the 21 claimed in many Voss biographies.

Aside from von Richthofen, Werner 'Bubi' Voss is probably the most well-known Fokker triplane pilot today, due in no small measure to his epic, and fatal, clash with No 56 Sqn. Voss was held in high regard by his RFC adversaries, and von Richthofen called him 'my closest competitor'. Some have claimed a 'fierce rivalry' existed between the two, yet in reality they were good friends. Von Richthofen had visited Voss's family in his home town of Krefeld, and even retained his relationship with them after Voss's death.

Both men had started their careers as fighter pilots in the prestigious

The famed fighting duo of Werner Voss and his Fokker F I 103/17. This aircraft was the second of two production triplanes allocated to JG I. Ltn Voss, the leader of *Jasta* 10, and a gifted and aggressive pilot, was the perfect match for the triplane's flying characteristics. 103/17 was fitted with captured 110 hp Le Rhône engine No T6247J, which had been taken from a Nieuport 17 of No 60 Sqn. Historians Alex Imrie and Manfred Thiemeyer uncovered the origin of the facial markings emblazoned on the cowling, which were based on the fierce features which adorned Japanese fighting kites. Due to business ties between textile manufacturers in Krefeld (Voss's birthplace) and Japan, a number of these kites wound up in the hands of Krefeld children (*A Imrie via VanWyngarden*)

Jasta 2, renamed *Jasta* Boelcke after the death of its legendary first commander; this was where they first met. Like the Rittmeister, Voss was a former cavalryman, a member of the 2. *Westfälische Husaren Regiment Nr. 11*, a unit known as the 'Dancing Hussars'. In *Jasta* Boelcke, the youthful airman scored 25 of his first 28 kills in just four months, earning the Knight's Cross with Swords of the Royal Hohenzollern House Order (generally known as 'the Hohenzollern') on 17 March. The *Pour le Mérite* soon followed on 8 April – five days before his 20th birthday.

Voss was a gifted, natural pilot, who was daring to the point of recklessness. Several German accounts state that on 18 March 1917 he shot down a BE 2 near Boyelles – his second victory within a few minutes. He observed German cavalry nearby, so landed his Albatros to seek some souvenirs from the BE.

Despite discovering that the cavalry were the last Germans to be retreating from an advancing British patrol, he still took time to wrench both Lewis guns from the BE and give them to the cavalrymen to turn over to a nearby infantry company as confirmation of his claim. He then set fire to the British aircraft and supposedly took off under fire of the advancing 'Tommies'. However, this story does not agree with that of the BE crewmen, who were both taken prisoner. The pilot had been fatally wounded, and his observer, Lt P van Baerle, recalled only that Voss strafed the hapless crew on the ground.

Thus, in the heat of battle, it seems Voss could be headstrong and somewhat ruthless. On one other occasion (5 June 1917) he is known to have strafed a downed British aircraft, wounding both crewmen, on the *German* side of the lines. It could be argued that he did this to prevent the crew from destroying their captive aircraft, but it may just as well have been youthful exuberance.

Voss possessed a cocksure confidence born of his young years and his considerable accomplishments, and seemed to care little for matters of military decorum. He could sometimes be found in a grimy drill-jacket without insignia, working on his aircraft alongside the enlisted mechanics. He could also be surprisingly impudent around superior officers, and this trait landed him in serious trouble in May 1917.

Voss was dissatisfied with the leadership of *Jasta* Boelcke's commander, the highly experienced 31-year-old Hptm Franz Walz. Together with another young ex-Hussar, Ltn von Lersner, Voss sent charges that Walz was 'war-weary', and unfit to command such an elite unit, to *Kofl* 2. (*Kommandeur der Flieger* of the 2nd Army). The ace's disregard for going through the chain of command, and for the military code of conduct, was viewed very seriously by the rigid hierarchy of the Imperial Army.

Walz was found blameless, but he felt dishonoured and his ability to lead compromised, and requested (and was given) a transfer to another unit. Voss was severely but privately reprimanded, and received the minor punishment of being 'demoted' from the prestigious *Jasta* Boelcke, in disgrace, to *Jasta* 5 – only his extraordinary combat record and his youth prevented him from harsher treatment.

On 20 May he was actually appointed acting commander of *Jasta* 5, and on 28 June was transferred to *Jasta* 29 as *Führer*. This appointment only lasted five days, however, for he was in turn posted to *Jasta* 14 as its CO. Despite Voss's rather nomadic command career, von Richthofen

was pleased to give him command of *Jasta* 10 at the end of July, and there his scoring streak was soon underway again.

On 6 September Voss was leading a group of *Jasta* 10 Albatros D V biplanes in Fokker F I 103/17 when they encountered a patrol of FE 2d two-seaters from No 20 Sqn, which had taken off at 1435 hrs. The FEs ran into Voss and his men above Boesdinghe, and Capt F D Stevens (pilot) and Lt W C Cambray, flying one of the 'Fees', described the action in their combat report, stating they had encountered '5 Albatros Scouts, 1 Triplane . . . painted light green'. They went on to state, 'The formation of FEs engaged 5 Albatros scouts and one hostile triplane. Almost immediately the triplane got on the tail of FE 2d B1895 (Pilot - Lt J O Pilkington, Observer - A M Mathews), who were firing at an Albatros scout which went down in a steep spiral. The FE immediately burst into flames. The enemy aircraft then broke off the combat and withdrew east'. Once again Voss's aim was true, and both men died in the blazing aircraft.

On 10 September Voss downed three Allied aircraft – two Camels from No 70 Sqn shortly before 1700 hrs (German time, which was one hour ahead of Allied time), followed by a French SPAD from SPA37 at 1815. No 70 Sqn's combat report clearly states that they were in action with a triplane and four Albatros Scouts. The next day Voss was in action again in 103/17, 'bagging' two more kills. His first action of the day, however, was with a Bristol Fighter of No 22 Sqn, and although his attack wounded the observer, the pilot flew his machine safely back to Allied territory.

Voss then claimed a Camel for his 46th kill and later, in the afternoon, he was in action again with Camels, this time from No 45 Sqn. This unit later reported a fight with a mixed bunch of Dr Is and Albatros Scouts.

This report reveals that the RFC were now aware that a German triplane was being met in combat, but not knowing there were only two

Mechanics from *Jasta* 10 pose with 103/17. The head of Gefr Karl Timm, Voss's trusted engine mechanic, can be seen poking just above the engine cowling. This aircraft was painted in overall undersurface light blue, with its uppersurfaces streaked in typical Fokker olive-brown (or khaki) of a rather greyish tinge, which produced a neutral overall impression. Note that the fuselage is already heavily stained and dirty, Timm recalled in later years how the oil from the rotary engine soaked into and darkened the forward fuselage fabric. He also recounted just how much effort he had to expend scraping off much of this oil, in a semi-hard state, from the entire airframe! The cowling of this machine may have been painted in *Jasta* 10's chrome yellow identification colour, but this assertion continues to provoke debate among enthusiasts. Indeed, it may have remained in factory-finish solid olive (Timm recalled doing no additional painting on the F I, and maintained it was flown as delivered), which would have provided a more visible contrast with the white facial features. There is circumstantial evidence for both opinions, but no proof of either possibility (*via A Imrie*)

Various dignitaries and JG I personnel examine Voss's F I during the visit of the Austro-Hungarian Crown Prince, Otto von Hapsburg, to Marcke aerodrome in early September 1917. Third from the left (far side) is the Prince, then JG I's adjutant, Karl Bodenschatz and Hptm Wilberg, Kofl of the 4th Army. Fourth from the right (with his hand on fuselage) is acting JG I commander Oblt von Döring. Note the fighter's white rudder, which was later presented, along with 103/17's compass, to A P F Rhys Davids as souvenirs following Voss's demise (*via VanWyngarden*)

such machines available, the British must have believed there were more. In fact, this might well be a case of Voss being so nimble and quick as a fighter pilot that his actions gave an impression that there was more than one triplane in the fight.

It must also be said that it was a frequent, and natural, occurrence for pilots on both sides to overestimate the number of enemy aircraft encountered in the desperate melee of a dogfight. It is also amusing to note that experienced RFC pilot Capt Norman MacMillan claimed *two* triplanes shot down 'out of control'! However, it was Voss who was victorious in this encounter, downing a Camel flown by another experienced British ace, Lt O L McMaking, who himself had claimed six victories prior to his death. MacMillan, on the other hand, survived the war with nine kills, and became a prolific aviation writer. This account of his fight with Voss, and F I 103/17, appeared in his book *Into the Blue*;

'Next day, in misty weather, with a patrol of seven, I saw a concentration of enemy aeroplanes some 21-strong flying below us east of Langemarck. There were three [sic] of the new Fokker triplanes, while the remainder were Albatros Scouts. They greatly outnumbered our strength . . . in any case I decided to attack. I dived on one of the triplanes, closed right in and as my burst went home I saw him falling down below his own formation. I knew that the Hun formation was so strong that it would be but to court disaster to follow him down. As I pulled forward from among the Huns for breathing space to review the situation, I saw that one of my formation who had followed me closely had done just the thing I knew was wrong.

'Engrossed in the shooting of an Albatros, he had passed right through the Hun level. Instantly, a Fokker pounced upon his tail. A burst of bullets caused the Camel pilot (McMaking – authors) to look round and swerve away from the Albatros he followed. I saw the triplane close in upon the Camel's tail, and I dived instantly upon it. As I dived, I fired a short burst before my sights were centred, because I knew that most Huns answered to the warning of bullets flying near. This fellow, however, was

15

Ltn Werner Voss photographed in a production Fokker V5 (Dr I) during his visit to the Fokker Works in Schwerin in September 1917. The aircraft has been fitted with a temporary headrest and increased facial protection for the pilot between the gun butts (*via VanWyngarden*)

of a different breed. He looked round at me and, as I saw his begoggled face above his shoulder, he swerved slightly to one side, then followed the Camel's tail.

'I think the Camel pilot was wounded by the triplane's very first burst, because he did not use the Camel to manoeuvre as he might.

'I increased speed and pulled closer to the triplane. Then I heard the splatter of Hun bullets rattling round my own ears. Glancing upward, I saw two Albatros scouts coming down upon me, but above them was another little Camel treating them the same.

'I was almost dead upon the triplane's tail when the pilot looked around again. The range was so close that I could almost read the man's expression. I gave him another burst and saw the stream of tracer miss his head by inches as he swerved outward from my line of sight. The Camel was below him falling steeply in a gentle curve. When my burst ceased, the German pilot looked ahead again.

'. . . Each time I had fired a trifle earlier than I might have done, in the desire to shake him off the Camel's tail. All the time we fell downward, losing height, fighting earthward from 14,000 ft along a pathway at 60 degrees, rushing through the misty air towards the ground behind the German lines . . .

'Out of the corner of my eye I saw a solitary RE 8 heading towards us. I followed the swerving triplane and got squarely on his tail. Before I could fire, he got out of my sights once more. Again I registered on him, dead. I pressed the triggers and saw my bullets flying home. His head did not look round this time. Suddenly, the RE 8 flashed in front of me between the German and my bus. I saw the wide-open mouth of the horror-struck observer. The wings passed across my vision as the pilot vainly strove to turn away.'

Macmillan pulled up hard and narrowly missed colliding with the RE 8 – by the time he recovered from his violent manoeuvring, Voss's F I and the Camel had both vanished. Unbeknownst to MacMillan at that moment, McMaking's Sopwith lay crashed on the ground near St Julian, and Voss was heading safely back to his airfield to report his 47th, and penultimate, victory.

KURT WOLFF FALLS

Kurt Wolff, commander of *Jasta* 11, had now returned to the Front, and he was keen to get his hands on one of the new triplanes – especially after hearing of Voss making light work of several opponents over recent days. Wolff had scored 33 victories with *Jasta* 11 and *Jasta* 29, had the *Pour le Mérite*, and was one of Germany's brightest stars at this time.

His name was as well known – and respected – by his foes in the RFC as those of Richthofen and Voss. His slender, almost frail appearance and modest demeanour had earned him the tongue-in-cheek nickname of '*zarte Blümlein*' (delicate little flower) from his *Staffel* mates – but in the air he was anything but delicate.

Under Richthofen's tutelage, he had become a masterfully aggressive *Jagdflieger,* whom JG I adjutant Karl Bodenschatz referred to as a 'berserker', or crazy man, in combat. On 12 September he was promoted to oberleutnant, but was not elated by the news – he wrote to his fiancée, 'It just depresses me that I am receiving this distinction now without having shot one down. Because, so far, I've had bad luck. I have already fought it out with about 20 Englishmen and haven't gotten one down'.

Wolff had been wounded in the left wrist back in July, and had not scored since his return to the Front. Even so, his 33 victories still ranked fourth among the scores of all living German aces at that point, after Richthofen, Voss and Gontermann of *Jasta* 15.

Therefore, eager to earn more laurels, and prove he deserved his promotion, Wolff flew 102/17 into heavily overcast skies from Marckebeeke airfield at about 1630 hrs (German time) on 15 September. It is understood that he was accompanied by a few of his pilots in their Albatros D V fighters. Some historians have suggested that he had already seen action on several occasions with the triplane, but in reality he had hardly had the time. Now he was flying the new aircraft, and he would see what he could do – it is impossible to be certain of just how much experience he had in the type by this point, however.

Four Sopwith Camels of No 10 Naval Air Squadron, led by Flt Lt D F Fitzgibbons, had been on patrol since 1515 hrs, and almost an hour later, they were shepherding some DH 4 bombers back to the lines. In the cloudy afternoon sky, Wolff became separated from his companions, but nevertheless continued on alone. At about 1630 hrs (British time) the naval pilots spotted the Albatros Scouts and headed for them, but the German pilots did not want to fight and dived eastwards. However, the Camels were then seen by the *Jasta* 11 pilots and combat was joined.

Wolff undoubtedly came across this action and joined in, and just like the Voss 'versus' No 45 Sqn fight four days earlier, the British pilots later reported that there were five Albatros Scouts and *four* Fokker triplanes! Reading Lt Norman MacGregor's combat report gives the impression that he attacked, and quickly despatched, Wolff and the triplane. Certainly this same report indicated that he closed to within 25 yards of the Dr I before before opening fire. However, one has to wonder if the 'four' triplanes, in reality, was Wolff flying like Voss – extremely agile in his actions, and occasionally going through cloud and emerging as if he was another machine entirely.

When he next looked, MacGregor saw the triplane going down in a steep dive, its pilot probably hit. He was only able to claim an 'out of control' victory (a probable), but Wolff was finished. It would seem that he had enough strength, or life, left to pull out of his headlong dive, as a photograph of the crashed 102/17 seems to indicate a less steep angle of descent. In the JG I war diary, Karl Bodenschatz noted that 102/17 had come down to the north of Werwicq (near the village of Nachtigall) and been totally consumed. The photograph, however, does not show the triplane as 'consumed', but merely smashed.

Wolff's death was clearly a devastating blow to the *Jasta,* the *Jagdgeschwader,* and to the reputation of the new triplane. While the great

Ltn Kurt Wolff, 33 victory ace with *Jasta* 11, was killed whilst fighting four Camels from 10 Naval Air Squadron on 15 September. He was flying new F I Triplane 102/17 at the time of his demise (*via Franks collection*)

aces were far from invulnerable from being downed in combat, the question was often posed – was he brought down by a better pilot, or in the case of a new aeroplane, was it the machine which let him down?

VOSS FALLS

Possibly with these questions still in the minds of JG I's pilots, eight days later another terrible blow was to befall them. Werner Voss was about to go on leave. He shot down his 48th victory on this morning of the 23rd, and now his brothers had arrived to accompany him home.

It would have been so easy just to pack his bags and go, but something delayed him. That may have been the thought that, with some hours of flying still available, he might be able to bring his score to 50 before leaving. Thus he had F I 103/17 readied for flight – by now its engine cowling bore his famous facial markings in white, based on the images which decorated Japanese fighting kites. It is currently a matter of fierce debate amongst enthusiasts as to whether or not the base colour of the cowling was *Jasta* 10's yellow identification colour, or factory finish olive-brown.

Voss may have recalled that at the end of April 1917 von Richthofen had been about to take some leave with his score standing at 48, and by the end of his final day at the Front he had shot down three British aircraft, thus being able to return to Germany with 51 kills. Voss was certainly capable of such things too. He had downed three on 11 September, and he was no doubt very aware that he had not made a single claim for the last 12 days since then.

A lone afternoon flight was made over the Front, and Voss ran into some SE 5as of No 60 Sqn. Despite being alone (although at some stage he was joined by a lone pilot in a red-nosed Albatros), Voss engaged the SEs and severely shot up two of them. As they headed down, Voss would be hopeful that their fall would be observed by German frontline troops, but almost at once he was faced with a seven-man patrol of SEs from No 56 Sqn's B Flight, which would soon be joined by elements of the same unit's C Flight.

No 56 Sqn was already known as one of the RFC's premier fighter units. Voss could not know it, but he was about to engage some of Britain's most experienced and successful aces in what became one of the Great War's most heroic aerial contests. The German's opponents would

The morning of 23 September 1917 saw Werner Voss (centre) pose for his final photograph, with his two elder brothers Otto and Max, in front of a yellow-nosed Pfalz D III at the *Jasta* 10 airfield at Marcke. Werner would be dead by sundown. His brothers later recalled how tired of the war their brother was, and how he was eagerly anticipating his coming leave, due to start that day (*via VanWyngarden*)

include (with their eventual victory totals) J T B McCudden VC (57), A P F Rhys Davids (25), R A Maybery (21), G H Bowman (32), R T C Hoidge (28) and K K Muspratt (8), amongst others. Even now Voss could – and perhaps should – have broken away and headed east. Many had done so before him, and no doubt the SE 5a pilots would have been unable to stop him.

However, Voss was an aggressive, even reckless, fighter, and his blood was up. Still keen to secure sure kills, he probably felt he could scrap with this lot for a few minutes, perhaps 'bag' one while they would be getting in each other's way, then hurry back home. He had drifted right over the frontline now, and despite his position being rather more precarious than at other times, he waded in nevertheless. For some minutes he outfought the SEs, and although he would never know it, his fire hit every fighter in B Flight – his accurate bursts had so damaged the machines of V P Cronyn and Muspratt that they were forced to limp home.

Eventually the unknown pilot in the red-nosed Albatros disappeared, and Voss was left alone facing six of the finest pilots of the Empire. The tale of the legendary duel that day has been retold many times, most notably in McCudden's memoir *Five Years in the Royal Flying Corps*. In fact, McCudden's account was so full of admiration for his skilful opponent that it was translated and re-printed in a number of post-war German books, including Bodenschatz's official history of JG I, *Jagd in Flanderns Himmel*. McCudden wrote;

'By now the German triplane was in the middle of our formation, and its handling was wonderful to behold. The pilot seemed to be firing at all of us simultaneously, and although I got behind him a second time, I could hardly stay there for a second. His movements were so quick and uncertain that none of us could hold him in sight at all for any decisive time . . . the triplane was still circling round in the midst of six SEs, who were all firing at it as the opportunity offered, and at one time I noted the triplane in the apex of a cone of tracer bullets from at least five machines.'

Then, inevitably, Voss was hit. Whether he himself was mortally wounded, or just his aircraft was damaged, will never be known. But he suddenly stopped twisting and zooming, and headed down in a glide. His propeller stopped, suggesting to some that he had run out of petrol – this may have occurred because he may still have been unfamiliar with the new machine's fuel duration. However, it seems unlikely a man as experienced as Voss would allow that situation to occur. Far more feasibly, either he was hit, and he quickly switched off his engine to avoid a fire in a crash-landing, or his fuel line was hit, stopping the flow to the engine which then fell silent.

As he glided down, Lt A P F Rhys Davids slid in behind the Fokker and gave it the *coup-de-grâce*. The Fokker fell to the ground at Plum Farm, north of Frezenburg, and just inside Allied lines. British 'Tommies', led by a Lt Kiegan, buried Voss where he fell. Unlike Richthofen, he would be laid to rest without a coffin and 'without military honours, exactly in the same manner as all soldiers are buried in battle'. His grave was later lost in the fierce turmoil of war.

After returning to their airfield in their shot up SEs, the pilots of No 56 Sqn excitedly discussed who the brilliantly talented enemy pilot might have been, and they were not surprised when it was eventually reported to be Voss. At JG I, however, nothing was known of the superb fight Voss had put up, nor of the dazzling exhibition of flying the triplane had displayed in his hands. The only knowledge they had came from Ltn Wendelmuth of *Jasta* 8, who tersely reported that Voss had been downed in an attack from behind by 'a Sopwith'.

The loss of two such capable and experienced pilots in eight days must have raised doubts about the new machine they had both been flying, but worse was to come.

MORE BAD NEWS

Examples of the production triplane, designated Dr I, became available in October. One of the first (115/17) was dispatched to *Jasta* 15 at La Neuville on the 4th for use by its *Staffelführer*, Ltn Heinrich Gontermann. A holder of the *Pour le Mérite,* Gontermann had achieved his 39th official kill two days earlier. Dr I 115/17 arrived at *Jasta* 15 on 11 October, but illness prevented Gontermann from flying it for two weeks.

Heinrich Gontermann was one of that rare breed among German fighter pilots – a balloon specialist. Indeed, of his 39 confirmed kills, 17 were kite balloons, which were dangerous targets due to their strong anti-aircraft defences. A native of Siegen in Westphalia, he had first served as an Uhlan (cavalryman), then as an officer in a Fusilier Regiment.

After transferring to aviation and qualifying as a pilot, he flew the Roland C II *'Walfisch'* and Albatros C I in *Kampfstaffel Tergnier* in 1916 before joining *Jasta* 5 in November of that year. Gontermann downed an FE 2b on his first sortie as a fighter pilot on the 14th, but his next victory would not follow until March 1917, after which he began to score rapidly. On Easter Sunday (13 April) he flamed his first balloon, and more soon followed. On the last day of April he was made CO of *Jasta* 15, where his continued successes brought the 'Blue Max' on May 14.

Gontermann's greatest day was 19 August, when he downed a SPAD, then later that evening destroyed four balloons in three minutes! The ace's letters home reveal a patriotic, deeply introspective and devoutly religious, yet fatalistic, character. On 25 March 1917 he wrote, 'Today I shot down a two-seater over the English lines. He broke up into dust in the air. It looked awful. It is a horrible job but one must do one's duty. Each time it is a victory for the German spirit'. Three days later, 'This whole aerial combat thing suddenly became much simpler for me. Now this means do not let yourself be taken by surprise, by ambition – besides, I fight for my Fatherland. I must do what I can. What will emerge from this is not my concern'.

On 10 July, when his score stood at 23, he wrote, 'Please make sure that people don't make such a fuss in Siegen because of my successes. It is all the same'.

Gontermann was delighted with his new triplane, but had little chance to fly it in combat, and the

His face smeared with anti-frostbite ointment, Heinrich Gontermann, leader of *Jasta* 15 and a 39-victory ace, received the first operational Fokker Dr I (as opposed to the F I types received by JG I) to be sent to the front on 11 October 1917. Although he was delighted with the triplane's qualities, he was cautious in his approach to flying it. Unhappily, 115/17 suffered structural failure of its top wing on 30 October and the balloon-buster was killed. This and other similar accidents led to an initial grounding of the new type. Note the fighter's unorthodox high windscreen (*via VanWyngarden*)

recent deaths of the JG I aces were on his mind. On 28 October he wrote, 'The day before yesterday I flew my fabulous triplane, but in quite bad weather. Hopefully, this crate will prove itself better at the Front than that of Richthofen's in which dear Wolff was shot down, and Voss who was also shot down in a triplane. Anyway, I will "put out feelers" with all my calmness and precaution'.

Two days later, Gontermann was test flying his new Dr I above the airfield at La Neuville. Despite his promise to feel his way with caution, his hopes concerning the triplane were not realised. Ltn Arntzen of *Jasta* 15 was an eyewitness to what happened next – he first observed the outer ends of the upper wing 'flapping' as the aircraft slipped to the left, then the right aileron detached, accompanied by wing ribs breaking away and fabric tearing off. Dr I 115/17 crashed and Gontermann was severely injured. Taken to the *Feldlazarett* (field hospital) at Marle, he died shortly after 2000 hrs. As the Germans were fond of saying, the great ace died '*unbesiegt*' (undefeated) in the air, through no fault of his own.

This must have been a worrisome time, for this same day Manfred von Richthofen had engine trouble, crash-landed and wrote off another triplane (114/17), just after his brother Lothar had also forced-landed with a sick engine. The next afternoon Ltn Günther Pastor of *Jasta* 11 crashed to his death when his Dr I (121/17) also suffered wing failure similar to Gontermann's aircraft.

Added to these tragedies, Vfw Josef Lautenschlager of *Jasta* 11 also suffered an ironic fate when, over Houthulst Forest, he edged too near a German two-seater and the observer, obviously thinking the aircraft was a Sopwith Triplane, opened fire and shot the unfortunate pilot down. His death, in 113/17, seemed like another nail in the triplane's coffin.

By this time Dr Is had been arriving at the *Jasta* 11 airfield in numbers. Seventeen arrived on 10 and 13 October, followed by a further five just over a week later. However, due to the fatal crashes of Gontermann and Pastor, all triplanes at the Front were grounded. Soon, an *Idflieg* crash committee (*Sturz Kommission*) arrived at the Front to try to discover the cause of the problems. Tests showed that the detaching of the ailerons was caused by weak attachment points collapsing under the loading imposed by a steep side-slip or bank. They also found evidence of glue joints in the top wings being weakened by a build-up of condensation within the wings, which pointed to poor workmanship and poor quality control.

Modifications and inspections were ordered, including a strengthened wing and redesigned ailerons. By 28 November 1917, Fokker was notified that the new wing was declared safe, and that deliveries could begin again. Despite the structural failures, the brief experiences the *Jasta* 11 pilots had had with the triplane were on the whole positive.

If the structural faults were indeed remedied, then the Dr I was still to be preferred over the old Albatros D V design and the recently-arrived Pfalz D III biplanes, which had also been found to be less than satisfactory by most pilots. Indeed, *Jasta* 11 pilot Richard Wenzl commented somewhat dryly, 'The triplane, the first of which came to the Front full of teething troubles, turned out to be a totally brilliant machine, since it no longer lost its upper wing'.

Staffel pilots liked the triplane's rate of climb and its manoeuvrability was superb. And while it was not as fast as some Allied aircraft, in close

Heinrich Gontermann fell foul of the triplane's early structural weakness before he could add to his 39 victories in the new fighter (*via Franks collection*)

combat following a diving attack, its pilot could often stay out of trouble with its quick turning ability. This capability was also enjoyed by Camel pilots, but whereas the British fighter turned faster to the left (the same way its rotary engine turned), the Dr I turned quickly in either direction. As one World War 1 pilot once told the authors, 'you had to really dogfight a triplane, and you had to be careful if you decided to break off combat, as the German pilot would nip in behind you in a second'.

Finally, during late November, remedial work had been completed on the triplanes, and those being built at Schwerin had undergone concentrated checks and modifications. The Fokker Company expected to deliver a further 170 or so triplanes during December, although in the event this appears to have been an over-estimate. A second production order for 100 *Dreideckers* (Dr I 121-220/17) had been placed in September, and a third and final order for 200 more (Dr I 400-599/17) was placed the following November.

The triplane was then considered the best German fighter in service, and was intended mainly for the elite *Jagdgeschwadern.* By the end of February 1918 there were 143 triplanes recorded at the Front, and the type's utilisation peaked at the end of April 1918, when there were 171 in frontline service (however, this number included those in storage at the *Armee Flug Parks* and at the fighter schools).

The triplane's greatest successes may have come during the great German Spring Offensive (the so-called *Kaiserschlacht,* or Emperor's Battle) launched on 21 March 1918, and the succeeding follow-up offensives. Formations of brightly-coloured *Jagdgeschwader* aircraft fought intense battles for air superiority as their infantry comrades struggled to advance on the ground below them. However, the day of the Dr I was brief, and the numbers in use fell off rapidly after June as the Fokker D VII arrived as a replacement.

This Dr I is believed to be 114/17 from the very first batch of production triplanes supplied to *Jasta* 11 in October 1917. JG I commander von Richthofen wrote this machine off on 30 October, when he was forced to make an emergency landing – it is thought he lost his cowling in flight due to the engine throwing a cylinder. As was common with *Jasta* 11 triplanes, the white square crossfields have been reduced with solid olive-brown paint (*via VanWyngarden*)

'RICHTHOFEN'S CIRCUS'

Jagdstaffel 11 was the most celebrated, and perhaps successful, exponent of the Fokker Dr I. There can be no doubt that its former leader, now *Jagdgeschwader Nr I* commander, Manfred von Richthofen was enthused about the nimble little fighter. Popular history would embrace them as a team, even though the 'Red Baron' only achieved 19 of his 80 confirmed victories flying the type.

Jasta 11 had first gained the appellation of 'The Travelling Circus' or 'Richthofen's Circus' from its respectful RFC opponents during 'Bloody April' of 1917, when the red Albatros D III fighters of the *Staffel* reaped a fearful harvest of British aeroplanes. The name probably originated from the British belief that Richthofen's 'Squadron' was continuously moved up and down the Front to wherever the German high command thought it was needed to combat Allied superiority. The fact that the unit also flew highly colourful aircraft may have helped to further implement this name.

The 'Circus' title was entirely a British (and later, American) one, and was not used by the pilots under Richthofen's command. Later it was generally – and perhaps more appropriately – applied to all of *Jagdgeschwader Nr I*, which truly was formed as a mobile unit. Within JG I, the red colour of *Jasta* 11 continued in use, and was typically applied to the cowlings, wheel covers and struts of the triplanes when they were acquired. Therefore, in the spring of 1918, when British airmen encountered massed formations which included red-nosed Dr Is, they usually – and often correctly – believed that the 'Circus' had arrived, and they were in for a hard-fought contest.

Manfred von Richthofen was not only a superb aerial hunter and expert marksman – he also excelled as a trainer, leader and motivator of the pilots under his command. Ltn Carl August von Schoenebeck, who was posted to *Jasta* 11 as a novice fighter pilot in May 1917, described some of the Rittmeister's technique in his contribution to the anthology *Flieger am Feind,* written in the 1930s (and translated by O'Brien Browne);

'How he took care of us beginners was wonderful, and what we learned from him! He himself took the training of each one of his pilots in his own hands. As soon as our duties allowed us, we had to shoot at a target. Everyone received 50 bullets each for both machine guns – and we beginners only made, on the average, from 50 to 60 hits out of 100. But the "aces" of the *Staffel* made 80 to 85. And when Richthofen came back, he almost always had over 90 – sometimes he did indeed place all his shots into the target!

'On the tenth day I was allowed to go along to the Front. Like a hen, he watched over me, the "chick". All of the beginners had to fly very close to him . . . every time when we returned he called us together for criticism.

And soon I noticed to my astonishment that, despite his life-or-death aerial battles, he didn't let us out of his view for a second. And this gave his *Staffel* a rock-strong feeling of security. Because each of us knew you could rely on Richthofen with dead certainty!

'The most vulnerable spot (in aerial combat) was naturally when one was attacked from behind. It was, therefore, much more important to look to the rear than to the front. This was the only crime that Richthofen knew – a hit from behind! After every aerial fight he went around each machine, and woe to us if he discovered a hit! Then you were really bawled out.'

Other members of *Jasta* 11 also commented on Richthofen's ability to keep an eye on every one of his pilots, no matter how frenetic the dogfighting became. He could also be a disciplinarian, and maintained high standards for the pilots of his unit. *Jasta* 11 pilot Friedrich-Wilhelm Lübbert recalled;

'Richthofen was very firm on one point – he kept in the *Staffel* only such pilots who really accomplished something. He observed each beginner for a time . . . then if he became concerned that the person was not up to the requirements that Richthofen placed on a fighter pilot . . . that person would surely be sent away . . .'

Von Richthofen had returned from leave on 23 October, having been sent the news of the loss of Kurt Wolff, Werner Voss and Heinrich Gontermann. Both of his November 1917 kills were made flying the Albatros D V, to which JG I had reverted while the triplanes were modified, and he did not score again during December, January or February 1918. He had been on leave again after Christmas, and for the whole of January he and his brother had been on a trip to Russia, then to Berlin. Manfred returned to *Jasta* 11 at Avesnes le Sec in early February, and Lothar was back by the 16th.

Despite *Jasta* 11 having been issued with a number of triplanes over this winter period, it is still difficult to know exactly who flew what at this time, as Albatros D Vs were still readily available. One has to imagine that the odd pilot might wish to fly an Albatros D V for a particular type of mission, and perhaps a junior pilot would fly an Albatros if there was no serviceable triplane available.

Manfred's younger brother Lothar had taken command of the *Jasta* following Wolff's death. He had 24 victories at the time, and before he too went on leave in January, he had increased his tally to 26. Meanwhile, the *Jasta* pilots flew Fokker Dr Is, Albatros D Vs and one or two Pfalz D III types, scoring the odd victory.

In what was probably the first combat success of the Dr I (as opposed to the two F I machines), Ltn Werner Steinhäuser flamed a balloon near Heudicourt for his

Ltn Werner Steinhäuser is seen swinging the propeller on what is believed to be one of his own triplanes, with another pilot in the cockpit. This Dr I bore *Jasta* 11 red on its cowling, wheel covers and struts. The faint eyes painted around the cooling holes in the cowling were probably applied in yellow (and no doubt inspired by Voss's triplane). The fighter's individual fuselage marking is thought to be a yellow 'X' on a red band – the two colours of Steinhäuser's former artillery regiment. Historians are uncertain whether these colours were also applied to the tailplane. This Dr I was equipped with two original-style ailerons that had the chord of their aerodynamic balances reduced. Note the mechanic holding the tail down (*via VanWyngarden*)

second confirmed claim. Unfortunately, on the same mission his *Staffel* mate Ltn Eberhardt Stapenhörst was brought down by ground fire in Dr I 144/17 and made a prisoner of war. His aircraft was the first entirely intact Fokker triplane to fall into Allied hands, and it became the subject of careful inspection and examination by Allied authorities (portions of its fabric still exist in the Imperial War Museum).

Ltn Hans Joachim Wolff had the leading edge and ribs of his top wing fail in flight on 3 February, but he managed to land Dr I 115/17 successfully and the aircraft was repaired. As March began three more pilots became casualties in triplanes, with one being killed in action and two wounded.

The men of the Richthofen *Geschwader* noticed a distinct increase in British aerial activity on 10 March as the RFC attempted to gather intelligence on the German build-up for the coming offensive, and the pilots of *Jasta* 11 responded. The brothers Richthofen were particularly successful at this time, Lothar downing a Bristol Fighter on the 11th and two more on the 12th, and Manfred claiming a fourth for his 64th victory on the latter date.

Manfred described his own aerial combat style as that first and foremost of a 'hunter' who carefully stalked his prey, but said his brother Lothar was a 'shooter' who impetuously charged into enemy formations with little forethought. However, Lothar's combat technique yielded impressive results – he attained his first 24 victories in a little over six weeks in his first tour at *Jasta* 11. Perhaps due to his impulsive tactics,

The youthful and earnest Ltn Joachim Wolff was nicknamed *Wölffchen*, or 'Little Wolff', by his *Jasta* 11 comrades to differentiate him from Kurt Wolff. Joachim, seen here with his pet (appropriately) wolf-hound, was an ex-Uhlan who had a troublesome start as a fighter pilot. Having joined the *Jasta* in July 1917, he was wounded on 14 August and sent to hospital. Back in action by February, he survived the structural failure of his Dr I 155/17 on the 3rd of the month, and finally attained his first victory on 18 March, which began a two-month scoring streak on the triplane. His tally stood at ten – most of them fighters – by the time he was downed, as Bodenschatz wrote, with two shots through his 'bold, tenacious, and bullet-riddled heart', on 6 May 1918 (*via VanWyngarden*)

Von Richthofen's 152/17 in which he scored victories 64, 65 and 66. It featured a red cowling, upper wing, wheels, struts and rear fuselage (*via VanWyngarden*)

Lothar would be wounded three times (each time on the 13th of the month!), which severely cut down his time at the Front.

In a post-war account, Lothar described his victories over the Bristol F 2B two-seaters on 12 March;

'Arriving at the Front, we saw about ten Englishmen heading for our lines at great altitude . . . to do their reconnaissance work. As soon as we reached their altitude – 5500 metres – we proceeded to attack. As always, my brother was on them first. He attacked one and forced him to go down. The Englishman tried to get rid of his opponent by diving and turning. My brother was always behind him. He then forced him, with more hits, to land the crate near our field. I looked around for a victim of my own.

'To that end there was one especially suited for me about a hundred metres below, beneath the English squadron. I attacked him. However, it was not easy for me. I flew ahead of my *Staffel*, which was only half as strong as the Englishmen . . . when I suddenly saw that I was surrounded by aeroplanes with English cockades. I made a long dive of about a hundred metres in order to get out of that unpleasant company. One of them had courage left over and followed me down.

'So now the fight was equal again. At the same altitude we flew toward one another head on. We approached each other with the great speed of 400 kmh. The Englishman had the advantage in that his observer could shoot at me the moment I flew past him. Here you must aim clean, otherwise you will get the worst of it. We rushed toward each other shooting. At the last moment I noticed I had hit him. A blazing aeroplane whizzed by me. A sea of fire in the form of the Englishmen whistled right by me. The observer stood up and stared into the flames. Completely ablaze, the English machine made another turn. Both crewmen jumped out along the way. This battle went so quickly that I shot down another from the same squadron and helped a third along . . .'

Lothar von Richthofen was shot down during a fight with No 62 Sqn Bristol F 2Bs on 13 March 1918. This picture of the crashed 454/17 emphasises the darker area around the aircraft's upper wing cross. The tail and top surface of the upper wing were apparently thinly over-painted in light yellow, although some of the camouflage streaks and the darker square cross backgrounds showed through the paint. Despite Lothar's exaggerated assertion that his 'triplane became a biplane', much of the upper wing structure survived the failure of the leading edge, and he was able to retain an element of control during his descent (*via VanWyngarden*)

By the time this photograph was taken the wreckage of Lothar's top wing has been removed, revealing the red cowling and cabane struts (*via VanWyngarden*)

The next day – the ominous 13th – *Jasta* 11 tangled with Bristol Fighters again, this time from No 62 Sqn, reinforced by Sopwith Camels from No 73 Sqn. Lothar's yellow-tailed Dr I 454/17 was hit during the engagement, with the triplane simultaneously suffering a leading edge failure of the top wing. His damaged machine staggered away and down, crashing badly, and the ace suffered severe facial wounds in the process. He later wrote;

'We had scarcely arrived at the front when we encountered a swarm of Englishmen. Everyone went down after one, and I did too. I attacked my opponent in a dive. Then there was a loud crash within my machine! It was hit. Only too late I noticed what was wrong. My triplane suddenly became a biplane (sic). It was a horrible feeling to be minus a wing at 4000 metres (he tried to get down, but was having great difficulty). With both remaining wings I could still bring it into a normal glide but only straight ahead, as the rudder no longer functioned.

'Before me lay a great open space. I wanted to land there . . . suddenly I saw before me a high-tension wire. I could no longer go over it and I could not get under it because two columns of men were moving along both sides of it. I did not want to take other people with me to the hereafter. Therefore I had to make a turn. But I was too low and it could no longer be done.'

Lothar's assertion that the entire upper wing had separated was highly exaggerated – numerous photos of the crashed 454/17 clearly show that enough of the main spar and ailerons remained intact to leave him some measure of control during his glide down, but the aircraft still crashed heavily. Lothar woke up in hospital with traumatic maxillofacial injuries, but survived to fly and fight again. He was claimed by the observer from one of the Bristols, and also by one of the No 73 Sqn Camel pilots who was firing at him during the same action – how much they actually contributed to his fall cannot be determined.

Jasta 11's triplanes are seen neatly lined up at Léchelle in late March 1918 (*via VanWyngarden*)

Photographed on the same day as the line-up shot seen on page 27, von Richthofen's 477/17 stands apart from the remaining aircraft in his *Jasta* 11. This aircraft boasted a red cowling, wheel covers, struts, top wing and, presumably, the top surface of its upper tailplane (*via Van Wyngarden*)

The Red Baron also flew 425/17 from Léchelle in late March 1918 – prior to the change in cross markings. Note the cover over the Dr I's propeller (*via VanWyngarden*)

Lothar was no stranger to injuries and hospital, and this time it kept him away from the Front until July. Oddly enough, he unknowingly achieved a measure of revenge upon his return to *Jasta* 11 – now flying a D VII, his first victory was a Camel from No 73 Sqn.

Manfred von Richthofen, meanwhile, remained in action at the Front as the great German March offensive began. Unquestioningly, he should have been relieved of combat duty, having been in almost constant action since the war began. He had still not really recovered from his head wound of the previous July, but his was a war of duty, not only to his country but to his pilots. Not that one would have guessed at the time that he was anything but an efficient fighting pilot – in fact, he was scoring more rapidly than he had since 'Bloody April' of the year before, and from all appearances had returned to his old form. By the end of March 1918 he had brought his score to 74, even scoring a triple on the 27th. All had been achieved in the triplane.

The Rittmeister's final two victories, bringing his score to an amazing 80, were achieved in classic style flying his all-red Dr I 425/17 on 20 April. The 79th victim was Maj Richard Raymond-Barker, a Camel pilot of No 3 Sqn who was killed. The last man von Richthofen shot

down was 2Lt David G Lewis of the same unit, who force-landed just minutes after Barker. Incredibly, he survived the encounter and enjoyed recounting the tale in later years – a native of Rhodesia, he outlived his victor by 60 years. Lewis is quoted from *Who Killed the Red Baron* by Charles and Ryan;

'Poor flying weather prevailed for most of the day on 20 April 1918, but at six o'clock in the evening it cleared sufficiently for two flights of aeroplanes – twelve in all – to take off. Some four miles behind enemy lines, at 10,000 ft, we sighted an enemy formation of 15 Fokker triplanes. When we flew past them and turned to choose our opponents, I knew we had encountered Richthofen's famed Circus. The Huns were painted every possible colour. Richthofen was out in front of the formation in his brilliant red Fokker.

'The fight had hardly begun when I saw Maj Barker's Camel explode on my left. An incendiary bullet must have hit his petrol tank. I went down on the tail of a bright blue triplane which crossed directly in front of me. I was about to try for a shot when I heard machine guns behind me. Bullets splintered the cabane struts in front of my head. I quickly forgot about the blue triplane and began evasive tactics. Glancing over my shoulder, I saw that my adversary was Richthofen in his all-red triplane.

'. . . I concentrated on keeping out of his line of fire. At that moment, Capt Douglas Bell – my flight commander – chased Richthofen off my tail. The tripe slipped down below me and I found myself in a good attacking position. He had become fixed in my sights and I opened fire. My tracers seemed to hit several portions of his tripe. But Richthofen was a wily devil and gave me the slip by pulling up in a steep right-hand climbing turn. Once again I was the target.

'He quickly squeezed off a concentrated burst and set one of my petrol tanks afire. I switched the engine off just before the Camel started to fall to earth. All the time sheets of flame alternately billowed up from my feet and over my body. The Camel slammed into the ground and I was flung about 60 ft from the wreckage by the impact.

'I was severely stunned, but lucky to escape without any broken bones. Maj Barker's aeroplane was blazing fiercely some 50 yards distant. I stumbled over to it but there was nothing I could do for him. I went back to my own flaming bus, and was watching it when Richthofen dove down to within 100 yards. He waved at me (or perhaps actually at nearby German infantry – authors) and I waved back. I then walked over to some German soldiers and surrendered myself. I was 19 at the time, and spent the rest of the war as a prisoner.'

The brothers Richthofen were far from being the only successful triplane pilots in *Jasta* 11, however. Ltn Richard Wenzl had been an Albatros D III pilot with *Jasta* 31 in 1917, and had scored one victory confirmed and another unconfirmed. His promise as an air fighter resulted in his transfer to *Jasta* 11, within JG I, at the beginning of April 1918. In his 1930 book *Richthofen Flieger* (translated by O'Brien Browne), Wenzl gives an excellent portrait of the atmosphere at *Jasta* 11 during this period. Here, he records his arrival;

'Just before (the *Jasta* 11 airfield at) Léchelle, as I was going up the slope to the airfield on foot, *Staffel* 11 was taking off in their triplanes. I will never forget this sight! I had already seen something of flying, but I was

Having already scored two victories with *Jasta* 31 flying Albatros Scouts, Ltn Richard Wenzl arrived at *Jasta* 11 on 27 March 1918. Upon his first look at the triplanes, he was 'astounded by the manoeuvrability and performance of these dreaded machines'. After taking a while to get used to 'shooting from this very sensitive machine', he re-opened his account with the destruction of an SE 5 on 16 May (*via VanWyngarden*)

astounded by the manoeuvrability and performance of these dreaded machines which were just then rising into the glow of the setting sun.

'On the field I immediately came across a couple of old friends, among them my high school comrade Weiss, with whom I had trained in Darmstadt in summer 1916. He had done well for himself, and by then had 12 aerial victories. I already felt at home.

'Richthofen had just taken off, so I could not yet report myself. After a short time he came back. He had just shot down his 75th, again in flames, of course. When he was in his "staff barracks", I went in to report. He was just at this moment deeply involved with a map with his adjutant Oblt Bodenschatz, and Léchelle already lay too far "behind" (the Front) for him. He wanted to see and evaluate the enemy aerial activity with his own eyes. When he saw me he said, "Well, we were successful after all in bringing you over here". After completing the official formalities, he said, "You are transferred to *Staffel* 11, and will enter there into a nice circle of comrades whom you will certainly feel good with. And they fly the triplane. There are enough machines there, and there is also no lack of ammunition – thus you have some chances . . .

'I was quartered in one of the Wellblech (corrugated iron, i.e. captured British Nissen huts) barracks which stood on the airfield. This itself was an abandoned English one, with four large tent hangars which most of our small machines fitted into . . . the barracks were really so mediocre that I had to wonder about the simple needs of English fliers. Because of the personal equipment of the Englishmen, which is really excellent, I had expected something different . . . all the barracks were basic: hot as soon as the sun shines on them, bitter cold when the night comes. There was no lack of cloth and blankets, which were brought over from the nearest storage house, and after two days my digs were quite homely. I shared them with Wolfram von Richthofen, the young cousin, who had just arrived.'

Wenzl first flew under Richthofen's leadership, and next under Ltn Ernst Udet, leader of *Jasta* 11, on 6 April. Wenzl commented that Udet was keen to go on leave to his fiancée in Munich, and also eager to score his 23rd victory to ensure the award of the *Pour le Mérite*, which was due;

'Udet . . . flew till his petrol tank was completely empty, until he finally shot down a Sopwith Camel in flames. Shortly afterwards, we got a Bristol Fighter in front of our guns. I raked up my opponent in an orderly manner, and he went down in a steep dive to a height of 200 metres above the ground, a few kilometres this side of the lines. My heart beat with joy all the way up in my throat – this fellow was certainly mine. Then he caught his machine, and as I was hurrying to quickly get him in my sights again, I suddenly vanished with a crack.

Ltn Ernst Udet, briefly of *Jasta* 11, ended the war as the second highest scoring German ace with 62 victories. The strain on his face clearly showing, Udet had just returned from a desperate combat with tenacious Camel pilot Lt C R Maasdorp of No 43 Sqn, who died after he was struck in the head by a single bullet. Udet visited the crash-site, returning with a blood-flecked serial number (C) 8224 from the wreckage. Udet undoubtedly marked this Dr I with his favoured 'LO' insignia in some form on the fuselage, and it almost certainly bore the *Jasta* 11 red colouring in the usual manner (*via VanWyngarden*)

'At first I thought that I had been hit by flak, but then it became clear that because of a sudden jerk, my seat had broken and I, together with the seat, was sitting on the control cables. When I could stick my nose out of the bodywork again, I found myself near to the ground, with the Englishman just swinging in behind me. So, with one hand on the fuselage I had to make, with the other one, an inglorious retreat.'

Wenzl survived this somewhat embarrassing episode, and went on to down an SE 5a on 16 May for his third of an eventual twelve confirmed claims. Of the flying demanded of the *Geschwader* pilots during the offensive, he wrote;

'Because we always had to be ready to take off, we had our flying combinations (overalls) on the whole day – the most some took off were their crash helmets for a short period of time. Hardly had the command to take off come from Richthofen, and he was already sitting in his aeroplane. It was at first (difficult) for me – and later for all new comrades – to first have to get used to this incredible speed. These first days rather exhausted me, even though I was an "old flier" – Richthofen demanded a lot.

'When the weather was good, there were not fewer than five take-offs (in one day), although I had personally participated in as many as seven. Added to this was the great manoeuvrability of the triplanes. I first had to get used to the sensitivity of the controls – my machine flew in much too unstable a manner, and banked too much in an aerial fight. After each landing, therefore, because of all the "coffee milling", I didn't feel quite the best. I cured my sensitive stomach with ample amounts of red wine and good ham sandwiches. The *Staffel* 11 Mess was, in general, splendid!'

RICHTHOFEN'S LOSS

It appears that moves were being made to end Rittmeister von Richthofen's combat days, thus forbidding Germany's greatest living aerial hero from risking death any further. He himself had refused such moves before, and certainly would not contemplate it now in the midst of Germany's greatest offensive in the West since 1914, when his presence at the Front was crucial. However, having brought his score to 80, he had agreed to take a brief leave and go hunting. As Richard Wenzl later wrote in his book;

'His leave had already been approved. He wanted to fly to Freiburg im Breisgau with *Wölffchen* (Hans Joachim Wolff, who was universally known as 'Little Wolff'), and from there hunt in the Black Forest. Everything was prepared – in case there was no flying weather – and even his sleeping-car ticket had been arranged.'

One might imagine that in his own mind Richthofen may have thought he could live with a decision from above that he stop flying altogether, if his score managed to top 100. He might

Dr I 161/17 was photographed with Manfred von Richthofen in the cockpit on a visit to *Jasta* 5 at Boistrancourt on 21 March 1918 – the JG I commander had just one month to live. This machine was painted in a manner identical to 152/17, with its red cowling, struts, wheel covers, upper wing and the tail, including the upper decking of the fuselage to the cockpit (*via VanWyngarden*)

425/17 is seen with its new crosses applied. This was the very machine that von Richthofen flew to his death on 21 April 1918. Here, the crosses look pristine, unlike the ones that were eventually taken as souvenirs (*via Van Wyngarden*)

then have thought that his duty had been done. This is mentioned as a possible motive for the several errors he made the following day – the fateful 21 April.

JG I had been asked to sweep the skies over the Somme valley, east of Amiens, so as to allow German two-seater reconnaissance machines to locate and photograph Australian field artillery positions somewhere to the west of the Morlancourt Ridge. These guns were a danger to a build-up of forces around Hamel prior to a planned attack upon the area east of Amiens. This mission dictated that the 'Circus' undertake offensive patrols over the frontlines, rather than the routine flights that typically saw pilots fending off Allied air intrusions over German lines.

On the morning of the 21st von Richthofen, flying his all-red Dr I 425/17, led a mixed formation of Fokkers and some Albatros Scouts over the Front, where two RE 8 observation machines of No 3 Sqn Australian Flying Corps were spotted. The red-nosed triplanes attacked, but one of the Baron's guns malfunctioned and he broke off. At the same time, the observer in one of the RE 8s succeeded in damaging the Dr I flown by Ltn Hans Weiss, cutting a rudder cable and forcing him to fly home.

Von Richthofen had had his left gun jam, while the firing pin in the other weapon had split, resulting in it failing to make proper contact with the base of the cartridges. It seems that this gun was jamming intermittently too, making it necessary for von Richthofen to constantly lean forward to operate the cocking handle. He had released his shoulder harness in order to repeatedly reach the handle.

Reforming after the skirmish with the RE 8s, the Fokkers then engaged Camels from No 209 Sqn that were out on an offensive patrol. The formation was led by experienced flight commander, Canadian Capt A Roy Brown. Well known today is the fact that each side had a novice flyer with them, von Richthofen's cousin Wolfram (known as 'Ulf') in a Dr I, and Wilfred 'Wop' May (an old school chum of Brown's) in a Camel.

Each of them had been told to stay clear of any close action, but they both waded in nevertheless. May appears to have attacked Wolfram, but then his guns jammed too so he headed for home. However, his departure was noticed by the Rittmeister, and he quickly dived after him, seeing victory number 81 within reach.

Von Richthofen now fell victim to several serious errors of judgement, and his cause was not helped by a change in the usual direction of the wind over northern France. This generally blows west to east, but this late morning was blowing east to west. German fighter pilots had often used the prevailing wind to advantage, knowing that Allied aircraft were usually 'helped' into German territory, and then had to struggle against any wind in trying to get home. However, on this occasion it seems the easterly wind moved von Richthofen more quickly westwards, and before he realised it he had crossed the Allied frontline and found himself over enemy territory.

Generally, German fighter pilots tended not to cross the lines except if they were attacking Allied balloons, or were chasing the odd two-seater at a higher level. Few would risk heading over Allied territory at low level. May had dropped right down to ground level in his haste to escape the attentions of the triplane, and was actually skipping over trees and areas of high ground. Von Richthofen, intent on his victim, but also distracted by his single – faulty – gun, did not realise his predicament until suddenly faced with two problems.

First was the approach from his left of a Camel – piloted by Roy Brown – which had headed down from the fighting above and was trying to force him off the pursuit of May, and secondly the approach of some higher ground where the Somme turned south.

Von Richthofen evaded the Camel, although the attack had caused him to lose position behind May's machine, but then he had to climb rapidly to crest the high ground. He tried once more to get on the Camel's tail, knowing that the second fighter had had to break off to the south as its pilot too saw the ridge coming up. However, von Richthofen's second gun now gave up, so the Baron quickly headed due east, moving over the Morlancourt Ridge as he did so.

By this time several machine gunners on the ground had been shooting at the triplane, and so had any number of riflemen. Australian troops held this section of the line, and an untold number of them were taking pot shots at the red Dr I. As von Richthofen crested the ridge, with some buildings and a chimney to his left (a brickworks), he was hit in the right side by a single 0.303-in bullet, which struck the front of his spine and went forward to exit just below his left nipple.

Realising that he was seriously hurt, he cut his engine, as any experienced pilot would do instinctively, de-pressurised his petrol tank and headed for the ground. However, von Richthofen's life was now ebbing away rapidly. He hit the ground, smashed the undercarriage and then ground to a halt. Within a few moments, just as a British artilleryman reached him, he gasped his final words and died. So ended the life of the highest-scoring air ace of World War 1.

Von Richthofen's errors this day had cost him his life. He failed to take stock of his location, and did not know, or realise, how far the wind was taking him, although he must have known (text continues on page 46) 33

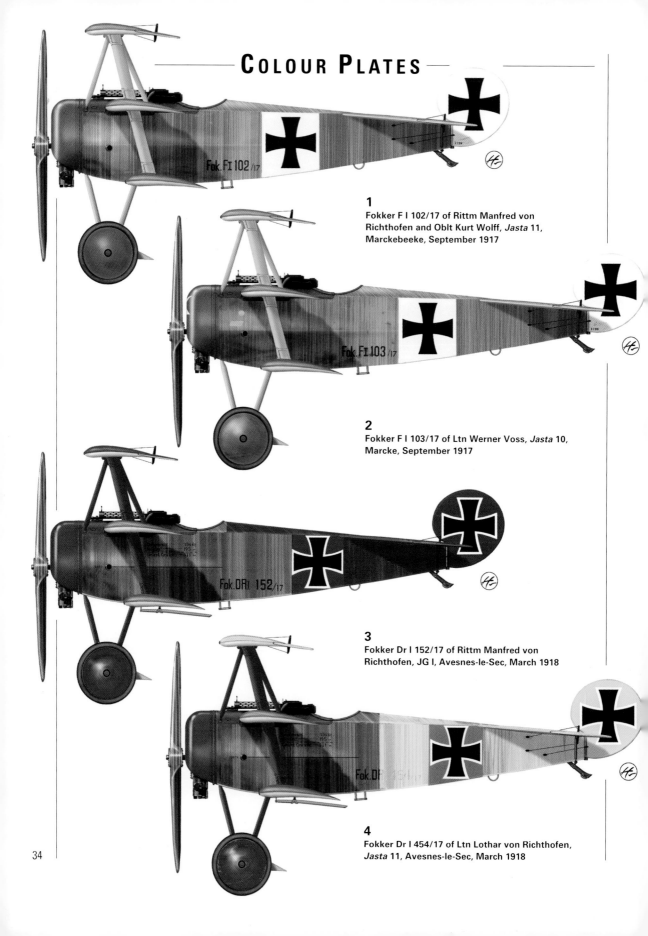

1
Fokker F I 102/17 of Rittm Manfred von
Richthofen and Oblt Kurt Wolff, *Jasta* 11,
Marckebeeke, September 1917

2
Fokker F I 103/17 of Ltn Werner Voss, *Jasta* 10,
Marcke, September 1917

3
Fokker Dr I 152/17 of Rittm Manfred von
Richthofen, JG I, Avesnes-le-Sec, March 1918

4
Fokker Dr I 454/17 of Ltn Lothar von Richthofen,
Jasta 11, Avesnes-le-Sec, March 1918

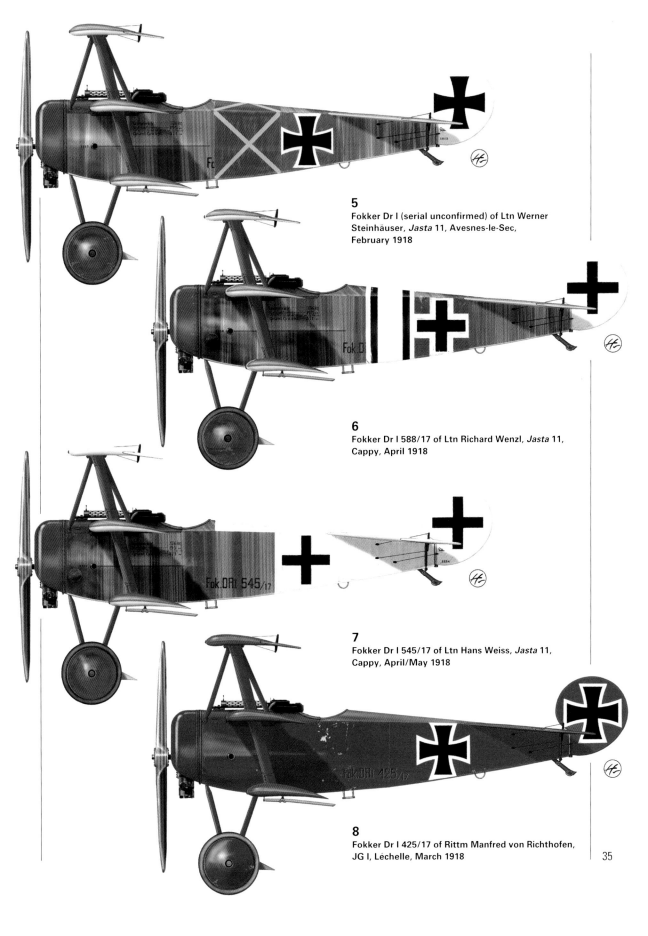

5
Fokker Dr I (serial unconfirmed) of Ltn Werner
Steinhäuser, *Jasta* 11, Avesnes-le-Sec,
February 1918

6
Fokker Dr I 588/17 of Ltn Richard Wenzl, *Jasta* 11,
Cappy, April 1918

7
Fokker Dr I 545/17 of Ltn Hans Weiss, *Jasta* 11,
Cappy, April/May 1918

8
Fokker Dr I 425/17 of Rittm Manfred von Richthofen,
JG I, Léchelle, March 1918

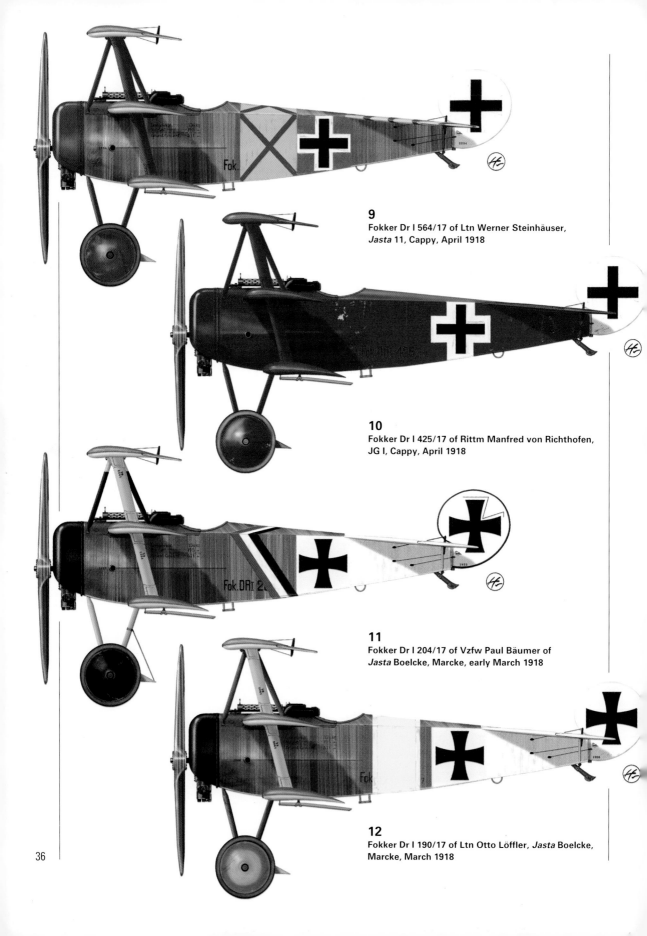

9
Fokker Dr I 564/17 of Ltn Werner Steinhäuser,
Jasta 11, Cappy, April 1918

10
Fokker Dr I 425/17 of Rittm Manfred von Richthofen,
JG I, Cappy, April 1918

11
Fokker Dr I 204/17 of Vzfw Paul Bäumer of
Jasta Boelcke, Marcke, early March 1918

12
Fokker Dr I 190/17 of Ltn Otto Löffler, *Jasta* Boelcke,
Marcke, March 1918

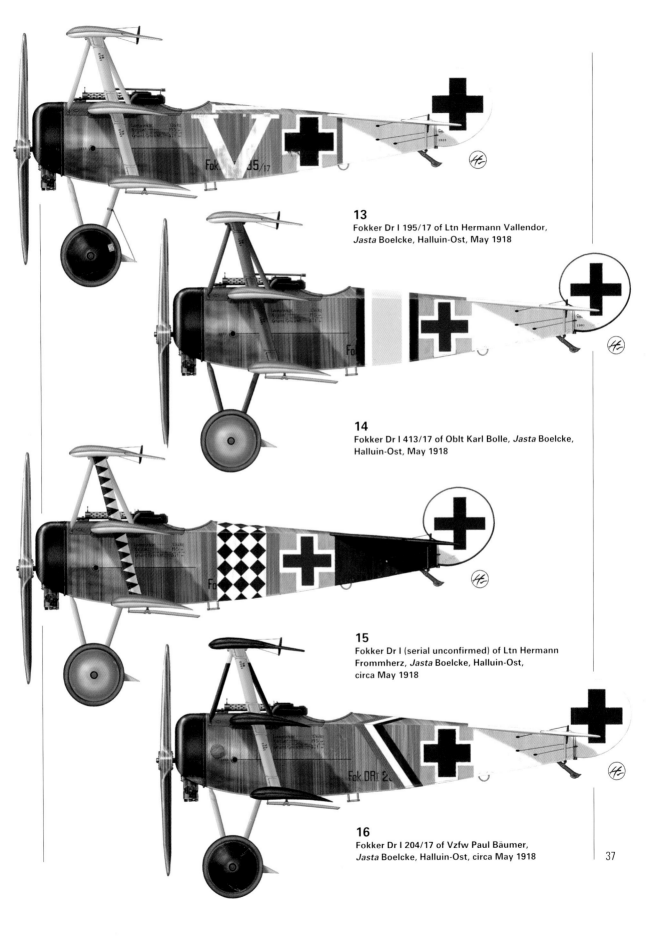

13
Fokker Dr I 195/17 of Ltn Hermann Vallendor, *Jasta* Boelcke, Halluin-Ost, May 1918

14
Fokker Dr I 413/17 of Oblt Karl Bolle, *Jasta* Boelcke, Halluin-Ost, May 1918

15
Fokker Dr I (serial unconfirmed) of Ltn Hermann Frommherz, *Jasta* Boelcke, Halluin-Ost, circa May 1918

16
Fokker Dr I 204/17 of Vzfw Paul Bäumer, *Jasta* Boelcke, Halluin-Ost, circa May 1918

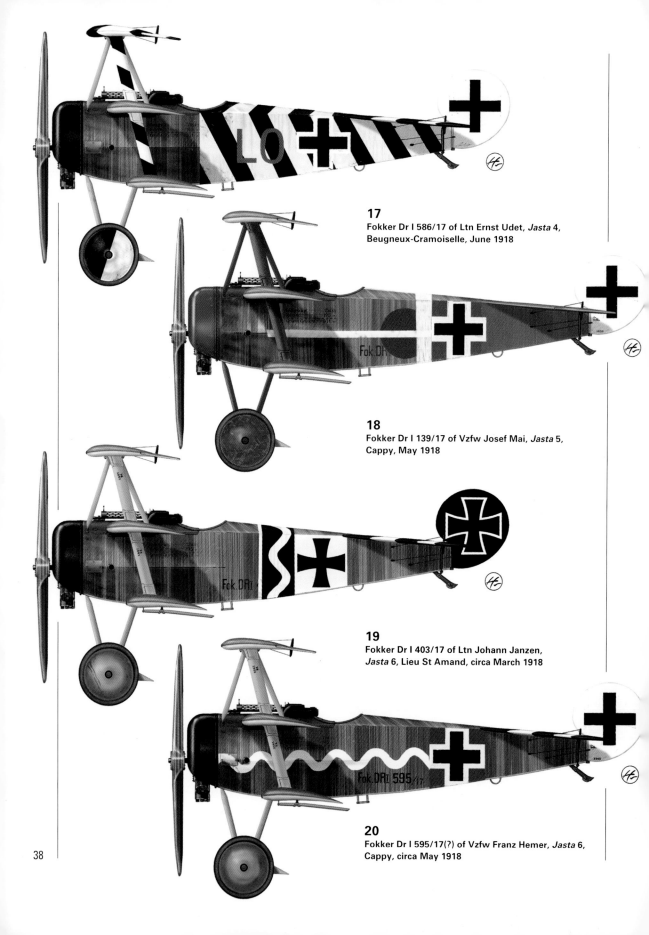

17
Fokker Dr I 586/17 of Ltn Ernst Udet, *Jasta* 4,
Beugneux-Cramoiselle, June 1918

18
Fokker Dr I 139/17 of Vzfw Josef Mai, *Jasta* 5,
Cappy, May 1918

19
Fokker Dr I 403/17 of Ltn Johann Janzen,
Jasta 6, Lieu St Amand, circa March 1918

20
Fokker Dr I 595/17(?) of Vzfw Franz Hemer, *Jasta* 6,
Cappy, circa May 1918

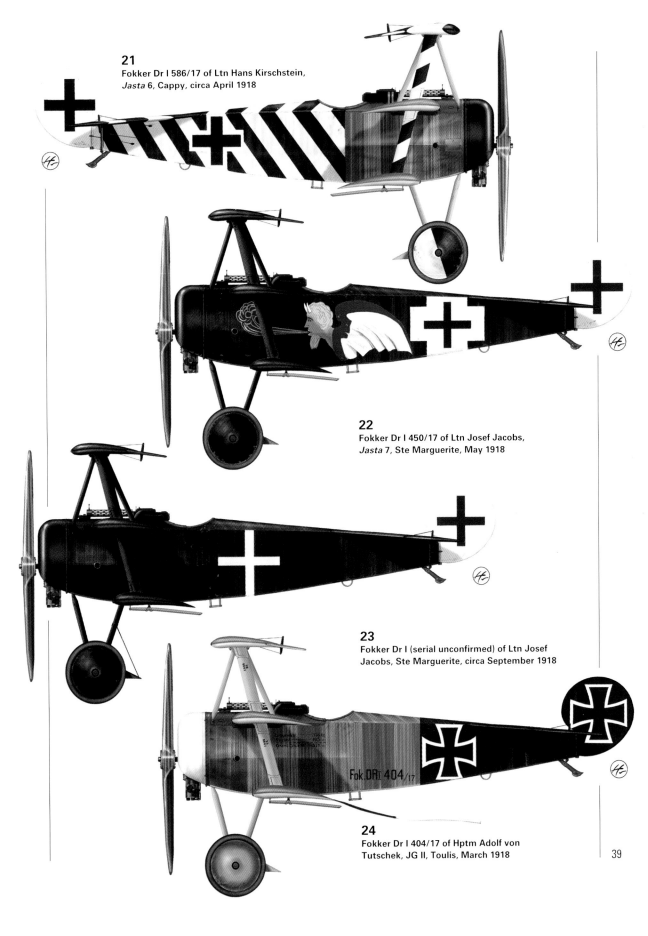

21
Fokker Dr I 586/17 of Ltn Hans Kirschstein,
Jasta 6, Cappy, circa April 1918

22
Fokker Dr I 450/17 of Ltn Josef Jacobs,
Jasta 7, Ste Marguerite, May 1918

23
Fokker Dr I (serial unconfirmed) of Ltn Josef
Jacobs, Ste Marguerite, circa September 1918

24
Fokker Dr I 404/17 of Hptm Adolf von
Tutschek, JG II, Toulis, March 1918

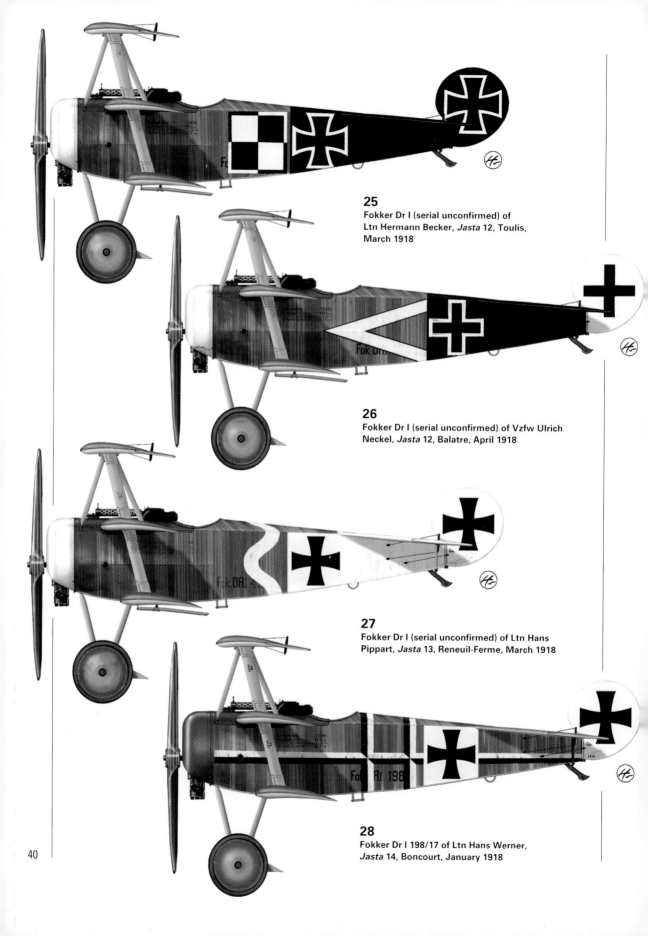

25
Fokker Dr I (serial unconfirmed) of
Ltn Hermann Becker, *Jasta* 12, Toulis,
March 1918

26
Fokker Dr I (serial unconfirmed) of Vzfw Ulrich
Neckel, *Jasta* 12, Balatre, April 1918

27
Fokker Dr I (serial unconfirmed) of Ltn Hans
Pippart, *Jasta* 13, Reneuil-Ferme, March 1918

28
Fokker Dr I 198/17 of Ltn Hans Werner,
Jasta 14, Boncourt, January 1918

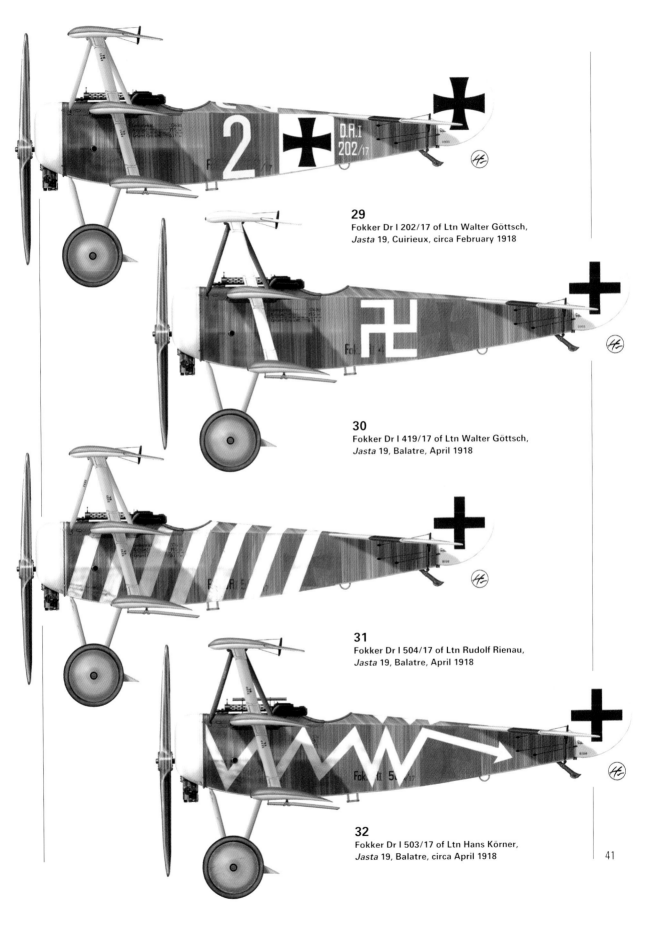

29
Fokker Dr I 202/17 of Ltn Walter Göttsch,
Jasta 19, Cuirieux, circa February 1918

30
Fokker Dr I 419/17 of Ltn Walter Göttsch,
Jasta 19, Balatre, April 1918

31
Fokker Dr I 504/17 of Ltn Rudolf Rienau,
Jasta 19, Balatre, April 1918

32
Fokker Dr I 503/17 of Ltn Hans Körner,
Jasta 19, Balatre, circa April 1918

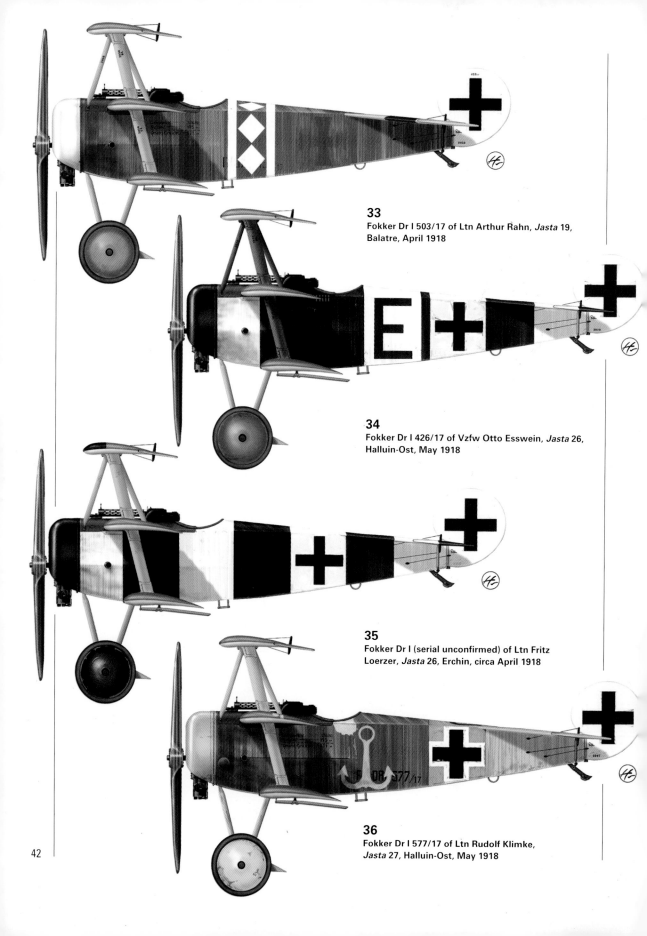

33
Fokker Dr I 503/17 of Ltn Arthur Rahn, *Jasta* 19,
Balatre, April 1918

34
Fokker Dr I 426/17 of Vzfw Otto Esswein, *Jasta* 26,
Halluin-Ost, May 1918

35
Fokker Dr I (serial unconfirmed) of Ltn Fritz
Loerzer, *Jasta* 26, Erchin, circa April 1918

36
Fokker Dr I 577/17 of Ltn Rudolf Klimke,
Jasta 27, Halluin-Ost, May 1918

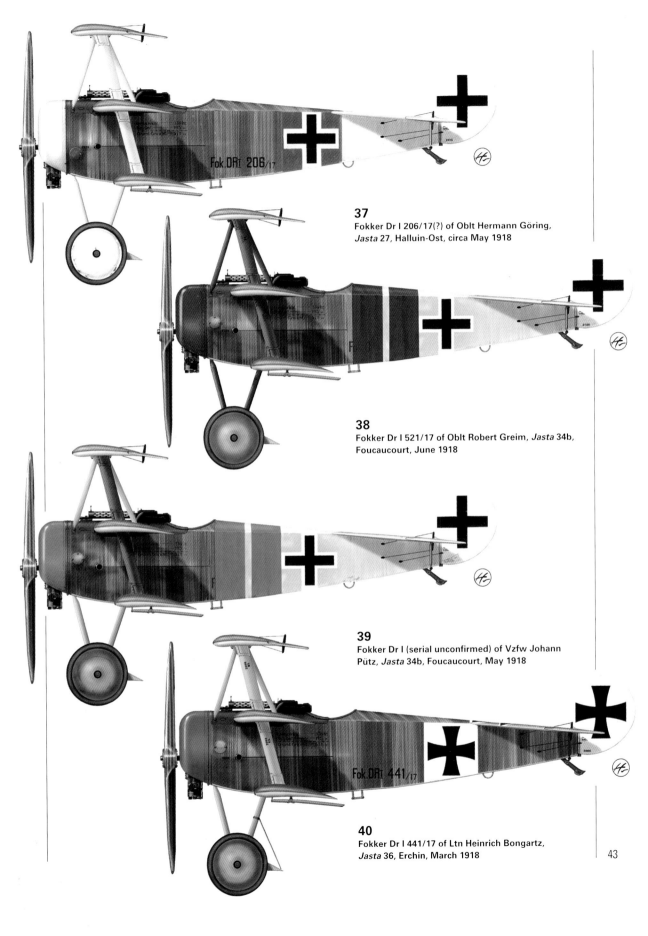

37
Fokker Dr I 206/17(?) of Oblt Hermann Göring,
Jasta 27, Halluin-Ost, circa May 1918

38
Fokker Dr I 521/17 of Oblt Robert Greim, *Jasta* 34b,
Foucaucourt, June 1918

39
Fokker Dr I (serial unconfirmed) of Vzfw Johann
Pütz, *Jasta* 34b, Foucaucourt, May 1918

40
Fokker Dr I 441/17 of Ltn Heinrich Bongartz,
Jasta 36, Erchin, March 1918

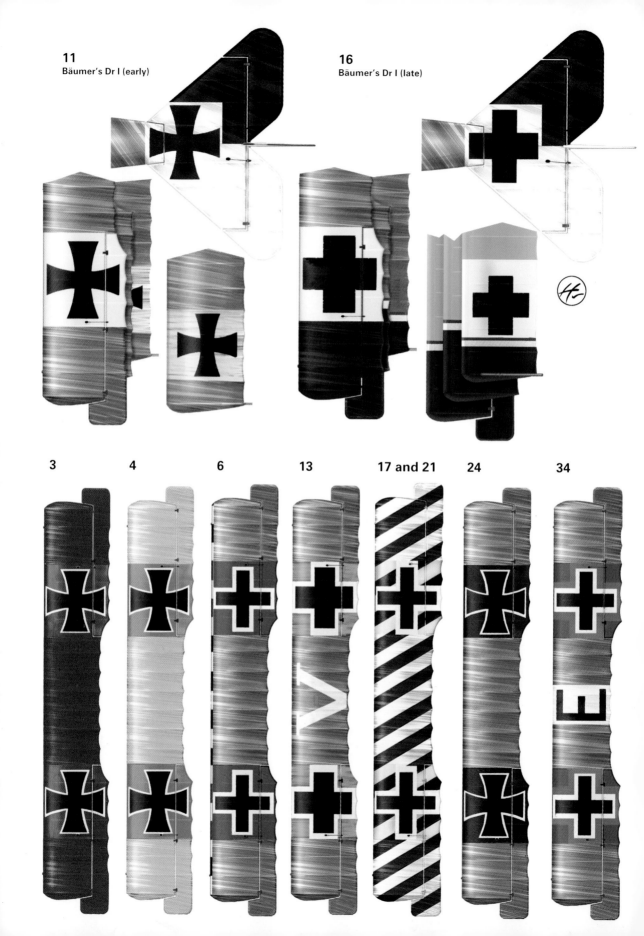

11
Bäumer's Dr I (early)

16
Bäumer's Dr I (late)

3   **4**   **6**   **13**   **17 and 21**   **24**   **34**

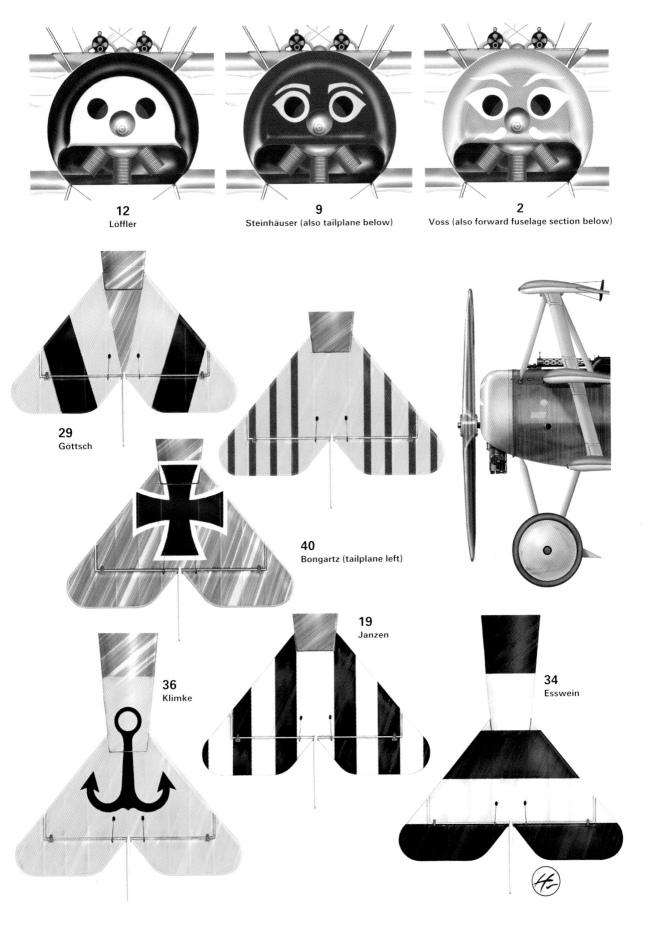

12
Löffler

9
Steinhäuser (also tailplane below)

2
Voss (also forward fuselage section below)

29
Göttsch

40
Bongartz (tailplane left)

36
Klimke

19
Janzen

34
Esswein

how close he was to the frontline. He allowed himself to become detached from his men, who would normally cover his back, flew too low and should have returned to base soon after his gun problems began. He chased an adversary for too long at low level with inadequate fire-power, and once attacked by Brown, he should then have broken away to the south, into the mist over the Somme, then turned east and home.

OTHER JASTA 11 ACES

With the Dr I in use for such a brief period in the frontline, and with imprecise records, it is not always possible to say with certainty how many victories a particular ace may have scored with the triplane. Von Richthofen is the exception because of all the research that has gone into his life, and his combat reports which have been preserved. We know he scored 19 victories in the Dr I, but it is difficult to be completely certain about other pilots.

Following von Richthofen's demise, ill fortune seems to have befallen *Jasta* 11, and a number of other aces of the unit soon followed their commander in death. One such individual was Hans Weiss, whom we have mentioned in the opening round of von Richthofen's last air fight. Previously with *Jasta* 10 (with whom he had claimed 11 victories), Weiss had only joined *Jasta* 11 on 1 April 1918. And it seems certain that he flew triplanes to gain his final five kills during April – four Camels and one Bristol Fighter – prior to his death.

Hans Weiss was born in Hof, on the Austrian border, in April 1892, making him almost exactly the same age as Manfred von Richthofen when he joined the 'Circus'. He flew as an NCO with various two-seater units during 1916-17, but in August he was posted to the Valenciennes *Jastaschule* (fighter school).

Bavarian Ltn Hans Weiss poses with his Dr I 545/17 at Cappy whilst serving as leader of *Jasta* 11 in late April 1918. This machine was marked with the *Staffel's* red paint on its nose, wheels and struts. Weiss's appropriate personal white colour was applied to the rear fuselage, tail and, supposedly, the top surface of the upper wing. After obtaining 18 victories, Weiss was shot down on 2 May by Lt M S Taylor of No 209 Sqn. According to Wenzl, '. . . Weiss was flying his new machine which he had had totally painted white'. It is possible more white colouration was added to 545/17 after this photograph was taken. In fact, Taylor's combat report simply described a 'white triplane' (*via VanWyngarden*)

Nineteen-year-old Edgar Scholz was called, 'our dashing Vizefeldwebel' by Wenzl, and he certainly looks the part in his fur-covered helmet and flying coat. The last of his six victories was probably scored with the Dr I in March-April 1918. Like Wenzl and Weiss, Scholz was one of the participants in the 21 April dog-fight which led to the Red Baron's demise (*via VanWyngarden*)

Six-victory ace Ltn Erich Just is seen seated in his *Jasta* 11 triplane. He was slightly wounded in the hand flying Dr I 110/17 on 1 March 1918, but remained with the *Staffel*. Soon back in action, he downed a Camel on 6 April for his second confirmed claim. Richard Wenzl wrote that Just was constantly playing the *Staffel* gramophone donated by the Albatros company, and that years later his ears still rang with the 'devastating' tunes from captured British records! (*via VanWyngarden*)

Triplane 564/17 forms the backdrop for Werner Steinhäuser of *Jasta* 11 at Cappy in late April 1918. Note that the fuselage cross insignia has been converted to the later *Balkenkreuz* format through the application of olive paint. The standard *Staffel* marking of red cowling, struts and wheel covers are also in evidence. Steinhäuser's personal red and yellow colours were applied to the fuselage band and tailplane (*via VanWyngarden*)

The following month Weiss joined *Jasta* 41, and by March 1918 had scored 11 victories, at which point he was assigned to JG I. His 12th was achieved with *Jasta* 10, and then he moved to *Jasta* 11 as a *Kette* (flight) leader, where he later served as acting unit commander. Wenzl stated, 'Weiss led *Staffel* 11 and did this in a superb manner – exactly like the Rittmeister, whom he had learned much from'.

A photo of Weiss in front of his Dr I reveals it had the usual *Jasta* 11 red cowling, struts and wheel covers, with Weiss's personal white colour displayed on the tail, rear fuselage and on top of the upper wing ('*weiss*' is German for 'white'). However, he may have added more white later, or even switched to a different 'all-white' aircraft by the time of his death, according to Wenzl.

Weiss was mortally hit on 2 May (von Richthofen's birthday), flying Fokker Dr I 545/17, in a fight with *Jasta* 11's old adversaries No 209 Sqn, and fell to his death at Meri-court. Again we quote from Wenzl's *Richthofen Flieger*;

'On May 2nd there was wonder-ful weather. Already in the morning there were strong scraps with the Tommies. In the afternoon, around 1430, we met, south of Albert, six to eight Camels. Weiss was flying his new machine which he had totally painted white. The Camels got above us – only Weiss reached this height in his wonderful machine, and was working over a Camel. Suddenly he was attacked from the side and above by another one and went steeply down, put the machine on its back, and crashed. A chance shot in the head had also taken this fine fellow from us.

'We were sitting in our digs under the impact of this loss when an ordnance officer came and reported that Scholz, our dashing Vizefeld-webel, had just fatally crashed on the airfield. That was a lot for this day.'

Edgar Scholz (also spelled Scholtz), who had probably scored one or two of his six kills in a triplane, had indeed died the same day as Weiss. This 19-year-old from Thuringia had first seen action with *Kasta* (*Kampfstaffel*) 10, joining *Jasta* 11 in January 1918 as an NCO. Scholz was lucky to survive one of his early combats in a Dr I when a falling Albatros Scout collided with his fighter, ripping off the tailplane. Somehow he had survived his own fall and crash. His luck finally ran out while taking off from Cappy, when he stalled Dr I 591/17 on take-off. The message promoting Scholz to leutnant arrived just an hour after his death.

The very next day (the 3 May) Ltn Erich Just was wounded in Dr I 110/17 by No 24 Sqn's SE 5a fighters. Just would eventually return and finish the war with six victories, one of which (a Camel) was probably gained with a triplane on 6 April.

Another *Jasta* 11 ace to die in June 1918 was Ltn Werner Steinhäuser, who was a close friend of Richard Wenzl;

'In Steinhäuser, I found a friend within a short period of time. He stuck to me not only in the air, but also on the ground . . . in every respect, he was a selfless, solid character – he always had a good sense of humour.'

A native of Konigsberg, Stein-häuser had previously flown in *Flieger Abteilung (A)* 261, where he and his observer had flamed a balloon on 20 August 1917 for his first victory. Steinhäuser joined the *Staffel* in December 1917, and as noted earlier, he had blooded the new Dr I on 13 January when he downed another balloon on the mission in which Stapenhörst's triplane was forced down behind British lines.

This better known picture shows Wenzl's machine, with its pilot linking arms with Steinhäuser in the foreground. Compared with the photograph on page 47, the Dr I now bears fuselage crosses converted to almost the correct specified ratio of 1:4, width to length. The serial number 588/17 was reportedly painted between Wenzl's personal black/white band and the lower vertical arm of the fuselage cross. Wenzl survived the war to write his 1930 memoir, *Richthofen Flieger* (*via VanWyngarden*)

21-year-old Ltn Werner Steinhäuser, who had been commissioned in the *2. Grossherzoglich Hessishches Feldartillerie-Regt. Nr 61*, achieved the majority of his ten victories as a triplane pilot in *Jasta* 11. He would fall during an attack on a French two-seater on 26 June 1918, and was buried two days later – 24 hours prior to his 22nd birthday (*HAC/UTD via VanWyngarden*)

Steinhäuser switched aircraft for his remaining victories, being credited with an RE 8 on 2 February for his third and a Bristol Fighter on 12 March in the same dogfight in which Manfred and Lothar accounted for three more Bristols. Five days later he was wounded in the foot and forced to make an emergency landing at *Jasta* 3. He was back in action by early May, downing a Camel on the 10th.

Steinhäuser's triplanes bore personal markings in the red and golden yellow colours of his old unit, the *2. Grossherzoglich Hessisches Feld-Artillerie Regiment Nr 61*. He would raise his string of victories to ten before being killed flying a Fokker D VII whilst attacking a French SPAD two-seater on 26 June.

Besides the renowned Kurt Wolff, there was another Wolff with *Jasta* 11 – Hans Joachim, aged 22, from Mülhausen. Like Richthofen, Wolff was a former Uhlan, and after transferring to the *Fliegertruppe* he had first served as a two-seater pilot in *Flieger Abteilung (A)* 216, and joined *Jasta* 11 on 6 July 1917. Just over a month later he was wounded by a Sopwith Triplane pilot of 1 Sqn RNAS on 14 August. He was back in action by late November, for he nosed over his aircraft when landing on the 23rd and was injured once again.

Known as *Wölffchen*, or 'Little Wolff', his first victory did not come until March 1918, when he shot down Lt A McCudden MC, the brother of Capt J T B McCudden VC. Wolff then began to fly the Dr I, and most, if not all, of his next ten victories were achieved whilst operating the type.

Wolff was an eager and high-spirited favourite among his *Jasta* comrades, including the *Geschwader Kommandeur*. He worshipped his mentor Richthofen, but he also enjoyed flying his Dr I in daring aerobatics when the Rittmeister was not around to witness them! Peter Lampel wrote the following impression of Wolff and Richthofen after the former had achieved his fourth victory on 2 April;

'"Little Wolff" (Richthofen) says, "I saw your victory. Can remember it clearly: a Tommy came along there burning downwards, and one behind him who was still slip sliding over one wing". He squints at him from below. "No, No", of course argues "Little Wolff". But then he says, "That was my fourth, Herr Rittmeister, and with that simultaneously the 250th of *Jagdstaffel* 11". Secretly, he hoped for a picture of Richthofen with his signature. But that comes only after the tenth victory – the Rittmeister is very stingy in this way. Then he hits him on the shoulder and his face breaks out in laughter. "Until you have left your laughable single-digit number of shoot-downs behind, 'Little Wolff, You still won't be a Kanone (literally "cannon" or "big gun" – the German equivalent of an ace)". But Ltn Wolff smiled a faraway smile. Great thoughts were floating about in his thick skull.

'Afterwards, he came late to the meal, with another gentleman. "Go in the corner", says the Rittmeister, "and eat your bowl of soup there, but with your faces to the wall", but after awhile, "Forget it!" All of the gentlemen received this well. There is a splendid spirit at *Staffel* 11.'

Joachim Wolff survived his *Kommandeur* by less than four weeks. He was killed in combat on 16 May, his victor being South African Lt H D Barton of No 24 Sqn. Wolff was his fourth victim (of an eventual 19), the RAF pilot claiming the Dr I south of Proyart. Along with *Staffel* mate *Unteroffizier* Robert Eiserbeck (killed on 12 April), Wolff was buried

Ltn Siegfried Gussmann achieved the 3rd and 4th of his eventual five victories flying the Dr I with *Jasta* 11 during March 1918. A leg wound suffered on 7 April kept him out of action for months, but he eventually returned to the *Jasta* and scored his 5th kill on 3 November (*via VanWyngarden*)

beside his *Jasta* 11 comrades Weiss and Scholz at the 'heroes cemetery' at Cappy, their four graves marked with a triplane's Axial propeller affixed to a wooden cross.

Oblt Erich Rüdiger von Wedel had been a comrade of Manfred von Richthofen's at the outbreak of the war, serving in the same Uhlan regiment (*Ulanen Regiment Nr 1*). Like his friend Richthofen, von Wedel was a professional officer. Posted to *Jasta* 11 just two days after the Rittmeister's death, he began scoring whilst the unit was still flying triplanes. By mid-May von Wedel had already claimed three victories, and in September he was given command of the *Jasta*. Made acting CO of the entire *Geschwader* when Oblt Hermann Göring went on leave on 22 October, he remained in that position until the final weeks of the war. Von Wedel survived the conflict with 13 confirmed kills to his name.

Ltn d R Siegfried Gussmann, a former observer on two-seaters, gained his 3rd and 4th victories flying triplanes in March 1918. Once, during a hectic air battle with British fighters in early April, a connecting rod in his Oberursel engine broke just as the attack started, cracking the cylinder open. Despite the possibility of his engine falling to pieces, Gussmann stayed and supported his comrades. He was wounded in the right calf on 7 April in a fight with No 73 Sqn's Camels, although he eventually returned to *Staffel* 11 and gained his fifth kill a week before the war ended.

Ltn Ernst Udet, the boyish, cheerful commander of *Jasta* 37, was personally recruited for JG I by von Richthofen on 15 March 1918. The 21-year-old Udet had already claimed 20 victories up to then, and he would soon receive the *Pour le Mérite*. A superb pilot and capable *Staffel* leader, Udet spent only a brief time with *Jasta* 11 – 18 March to 8 April – but in that eventful period shot down three Allied aircraft.

In his first sortie in a Dr I he shot down an RE 8, attacking it from the front. His flight, which was being led by von Richthofen, then proceeded to strafe British troops on the ground. In his book *Mein Fliegerleben* Udet wrote;

'Richthofen, the steel point of our wedge formation, continues in a steep glide towards the Roman road. At a height of about ten metres he races along the ground, both machine guns firing without letup into the marching columns on the road. We stay behind him and pour out more fire.

'A paralysing terror seems to have seized the troops – only a few make the ditches. Most fall where they walk or stand. At the end of the road (von Richthofen) makes a tight turn and proceeds with another pass along the treetops. Now we can clearly observe the effect of our first strafing run – bolting horse teams, abandoned guns which, like breakwaters, stem the oncoming human flood.

'This time we receive some return fire from below. Infantrymen stand there, rifles pressed to the cheek, and from a ditch a machine gun barks up at us. But (Richthofen) does not come up a single metre because of this, even though his wings are taking bullet holes.'

After this flight Udet was made CO of *Jasta* 11, and he downed two Camels within a few days. One fell on 28 March, Udet later recording;

'An Englishman is above us and he comes down on Gussmann who avoids him by diving. I lift my head for a moment and see a second Englishman making for me – he is barely 50 metres off. At 80 metres he opens fire. It is impossible to avoid him, so I go straight towards him. We are 20 metres apart, and it looks as though we will ram each other in another second. Then, a small movement, and he barely skims over me. His propwash shakes me and the smell of castor oil flows past me.

'Another bank. Again he is straight across from me and once more we go for each other. The thin white trails of the tracers hang in the air like curtains. He skims over me with barely a hand's width to spare . . . "8224" it reads on his fuselage in black numerals.

'The fourth time I can feel my hands becoming damp. It is him or me – one of us has to go. I line him up in my sights and go for him, resolved not to give an inch. He turns to avoid me and is caught by my burst. His aircraft rears up, turns on its back and disappears in a gigantic crater. A fountain of earth and smoke. I fly home, soaked through, and my nerves are still vibrating.'

That evening Udet went to a nearby field hospital where his victim's body had been taken. The Allied pilot had received a head shot and been killed instantly. The doctor handed Udet the dead man's visiting card, upon which was printed, 'Lt C R Maasdorp, Ontario, RFC'. There was also a photograph of the pilot's mother and a letter. One line read, 'You mustn't fly so many sorties. Think of your father and me'.

Shortly afterwards, on 8 April, Udet was taken out of action by a painful ear infection (a common problem for pilots in open-cockpit aircraft). He left for leave, and possible hospitalisation, although he returned in late May and took command of *Jasta* 4, where he continued to fly the Dr I. During another leave in the summer of 1918, Udet dictated a brief book entitled *Kreuz wider Kokarde* (*Cross against Cockade*, edited by Ernst Eichler), which contains the usual wartime propaganda (especially about the 'fast' Fokker triplanes!) and censorship, but which also records the following evocative passages about his time in *Jasta* 11;

'. . . Richthofen told me that he needed one more *Staffelführer* for his *Geschwader*, and he offered the post to me. I was naturally burning (with desire) for this, to be allowed to work under him, and after three days I was already *Staffelführer* at the *Geschwader* Richthofen. I could now fly at the Front with the man who was admired by all of Germany.

'His flying ability was amazing. I had, during the many flights to the Front which I made with him, only one single time observed that an opponent escaped from him. He left all enemy aeroplanes he encountered in flames. He said that in his view this was the only real way to shoot someone down.

'Usually, we flew as eight or ten aeroplanes, and used the extraordinarily fast Fokker triplane with a rotary engine – the best machine available for aerial combat. During the first days of the offensive, the *Geschwader* really wreaked havoc among our opponents – on one day 12 Englishmen were shot down by us alone. Richthofen always participated in two or three victories. In good weather he flew four to five times a day. He only took breaks to eat or sleep.

'Richthofen was a soldier through and through. One noticed this when flying, for he always directed the main focus of his attention on using his troops, and bagging enemy fliers. Only when he didn't receive something good to eat was he in a bad mood. His life in the field consisted of flying, sleeping and eating.

'During the first days of the latest big offensive, bad, rainy weather ruled. The cloud layer pushed down to 400 metres. Accordingly, aerial activity was also limited to this low height, with aerial combat being played out as a rule between 100 and 200 metres above the ground. The English single- and two-seaters were being mainly used against ground targets. One must say that they attempted to complete their tasks with quite superb dash – and some-times they succeeded.

Manfred von Richthofen achieved his 71st, 74th and 76th victories flying Dr I 127/17, and it was described in his combat reports as having the standard colour scheme for his 'reserve' triplanes – red tail, cowling, wheels and top wing uppersurface. This photo pre-dates this decoration, and only the rudder has been thinly over-painted in 'streaky' olive to leave a white outline in typical *Jasta* 11 style for this period. The identity of the triplane's occupant in this photograph remains unknown (*via VanWyngarden*)

'I remember several cases where the English aeroplanes showed an extraordinary boldness – we were once flying with around six aeroplanes, the Rittmeister at the head, along the front from "A" to the south, at a height of about 300 metres. South of us three two-seaters were moving, flying along a road at a height of nearly 50 metres, and shooting at our columns which were marching forward. Two turned around and flew in a south-westerly direction to their side, while the other one did not let itself be influenced by our attentions and rather quickly dropped four bombs next to the heavily occupied road. The next moment, he had been shot down in flames by Richthofen. This was an Armstrong two-seater. With a powerful explosion, it immediately hit near the road that it had been attacking.

'The field-greys (German infantry) waved their hands to us in thanks as we circled over the opponent . . . because at around 200 metres above us five Englishmen showed themselves again. We pulled our triplanes upward and, after a minute, we were behind them – one of them, a Bristol two-seater, performed a clean bank over our heads and came down on us with a scream. He would have to attack Richthofen with his fixed machine gun. In four seconds the picture had quite changed and the dashing Bristol two-seater roared down burning in many pieces in a field, around 200 metres near the first victory site. In the afternoon of the same day, Richthofen shot down his third in flames. After that he decided, as an exception, to drop his usual "evening take off".'

The last paragraph is apparently describing the events of 27 March, when the Rittmeister recorded his 71st through 73rd victories. However, as Udet was dictating these incidents entirely from memory, he appears to have confused the sequence and details. Recent research shows that Richthofen actually downed a Camel *first*, then an Armstrong-Whitworth FK 8 two-seater and then a Sopwith Dolphin!

Jasta 11 went through some lean times following the deaths of Weiss, Scholz, Wolff, and Eiserbeck, and the wounding of Just. Wenzl recorded that in early May he was the only pilot from the *Staffel* available for flying, and that sometimes the few *Jasta* 11 pilots flew as a unit with *Jasta* 4 or 6. However, as May wore on the personnel shortage improved and – finally – the Fokker D VII began to arrive in quantity. By early June the *Staffel* pilots had gladly relinquished their triplanes for the new biplane Fokkers.

Richard Wenzl's triplane (reportedly 588/17) shows off the black and white stripes on the leading edges of its wings. He has also applied his personal black/white fuselage marking band based on the Iron Cross ribbon (with the colours reversed). Wenzl had previously used this marking on his Albatros when serving with *Jasta* 31, and continued its use on his later Fokker D VII and E V. This Dr I displays the 'thick' form of *Balkenkreuz* first used on *Jasta* 11 triplanes, and also features a red engine cowling, wheels and struts. The machine in the background is one of von Richthofen's all-red Dr Is, most likely 152/17 (*via VanWyngarden*)

MARKINGS

More often than not, *Jasta* aircraft were identified by one or more colours applied to a specific portion of the airframe such as the nose, fuselage and/or the tail section. Individual pilots were recognised in the air by an assortment of insignia, including letters, numbers, pictorial symbols or emblems, or a coloured nose or tail.

Since taking over *Jasta* 11, von Richthofen had used the colour red as a personal identifying scheme. Later, most *Jasta* aircraft carried red colouring as well, and by the summer of 1917 this had been standardised to a unit marking of a red nose, struts and wheel covers on the unit's Albatros fighters. Von Richthofen himself stated that the tailplanes and elevators were the best location for individual colours, and many aircraft in the unit were so marked.

Others displayed their personal markings on the fuselage between the cockpit and the national insignia – the black and white chequered band of Stapenhörst's Dr I 144/17 is well known, and Richard Wenzl was quick to mark his triplane with his usual 'reverse E. K. (*Eiserne Kreuz*) band', which took the form of a vertical black and white band in the

This rear-view of Wenzl's Dr I shows the method of marking the early *Balkenkreuz* insignia on the wings and now white rudder (*via VanWyngarden*)

proportions of the medal ribbon for the Iron Cross, but with the black and white colours reversed.

When the triplanes arrived from the factory, their upper surfaces were finished with standard Fokker greenish-brown 'streaked' camouflage applied over clear-doped fabric. These streaks were just slightly oblique on the wing surfaces, vertical on the sides of the fuselage and diagonally brushed on the fuselage decking and tailplane/elevators. The cowlings were generally painted solid greenish (olive) brown, whilst the undersurfaces were finished in a light greyish-blue – a thin 'border' of which appeared on the bottom of the fuselage and around the tailplane.

The national insignia iron crosses were applied on white square fields and on a white rudder, which was very much an out-of-date application by this time. At *Jasta* 11 the white cross fields were frequently painted over with a solid olive-brown camouflage colour, leaving the proper regulation five-centimetre white border. Occasionally, this was even done on the rudder, where it was not specified.

On 17 March 1918 a new *Idflieg* instruction specified that the iron crosses were to be replaced by *Balkenkreuze*, or straight-sided insignia, with a 15-cm white border on the wings and fuselage. Further modifications to this insignia followed, and the photographs published in this book reveal a wide range of styles and applications.

Von Richthofen flew several different triplanes, all of which were marked differently. Although there are many references to him always flying a pure red triplane, he reportedly only flew this machine during major ground offensives. This was for two reasons. Firstly, to ensure his pilots could quickly spot him during combat, and secondly, so that ground observers (air defence officers) could readily identify his aircraft to provide confirmation of his victories.

Peter Lampel stated that Richthofen's 'reserve' triplane had red wings, along with the usual red cowling which all of the *Staffel* aircraft displayed. This is an obvious simplification, for photographs show that Dr Is 152/17 and 161/17 had not only a red top surface to the upper wing, but a red tail, rudder, rear fuselage and top decking up to the cockpit. It would appear that some of the Rittmeister's other machines – 127/17 and 477/17 – were similarly painted. However, at some point 477/17 was painted red overall, as was 425/17. When the *Balkenkreuz* form of insignia were applied, the rudders of these red machines were painted white. Incidentally, Lampel also stated that both the Rittmeister's machines carried two leader's streamers – an aspect not apparent in available photos.

One of the *Balkenkreuz* insignia from von Richthofen's 425/17, which is now the property of the Royal Canadian Military Institute in Toronto. Presented to the institute by Capt Roy Brown after World War 1, the centre area has been cut out, and in its place are the signatures of No 209 Sqn pilots on strength in late April 1918. Ironically, Roy Brown's monicker is missing, for he had already left the unit by then (*via Franks collection*)

A FIGHTER FOR THE CHOSEN FEW

O f the 80 or so *Jagdstaffeln* which eventually made up most of the German fighter forces in 1918, only about 14 are known to have been equipped with the Fokker Dr I in quantity. Nearly all of these were component units of the elite *Jagdgeschwadern* I, II and III. These were permanent groupings of four *Staffeln* each, created as mobile formations able to move quickly to wherever the fighting was most intense – usually as part of an offensive.

The Dr I was considered the best German fighter available in early 1918, hence its allocation as *Geschwader* equipment. As we have seen, *Jasta* 11 was the first element of JG I to receive the type, and *Jagdstaffeln* 4 and 6 would also fly the triplane (*Jasta* 10 pilots, in general, retained their Pfalz D IIIa and Albatros D Va biplanes in anticipation of getting the first Fokker D VIIs). Within JG II, *Jagdstaffeln* 12, 13 and 19 would eventually operate triplanes, whilst all four component units of JG III (*Jagdstaffeln* Boelcke, 26, 27 and 36) would fly the Dr I in some numbers.

In this chapter we will look at the aces of each of these units – and a few others – who achieved a degree of success on the Fokker Dr I.

──── JASTA BOELCKE ────

Jasta 2 had been known as *Jasta* Boelcke (or simply *Jasta* B) since the death of its first commander, Oswald Boelcke, in October 1916, and it was a prestigious *Staffel* which would finish the war second only to *Jasta* 11 in its number of confirmed victories (333 aircraft and three balloons). Many of the great aces served with this unit, although as the war progressed it went through leaner times in terms of combat successes.

It may be said that the *Staffel* endured something of a scoring slump in the summer of 1917, then slowly began to regain its former reputation. However, in the period from late November 1917 through to early January 1918, it lost three succeeding commanders – all *Pour le Mérite* winners – killed in action. With the entry of Ltn Karl Bolle as *Staffelführer* in February 1918, along with the acquisition of the Dr I, the unit hit its stride again as its new CO strove to re-instill the spirit of Boelcke into his men.

It is stressed again that due to poor records, and the limited time the Dr I was in combat, it may not be possible to say with any certainty that a particular pilot scored five or more victories on the type, even though the individual ace may have had a high score overall. Therefore, it must be remembered that we shall be noting aces who flew the triplane, and not necessarily pilots who attained five or more victories on the type.

On New Year's Day 1918, a Fokker D V arrived at *Jasta* Boelcke's field at Bavichove – the D V was a rotary-engined biplane trainer, and was issued to units so that pilots could accustom themselves to operating the Oberursel engine prior to the arrival of the Dr Is. On 10 January 1918

Karl Bolle of *Jasta* Boelcke ended the war with 36 victories, and the 'Blue Max' (*via Franks collection*)

Jasta B received its first three examples of the triplane from the 4th Army *AFP* in Ghent. Anthony Fokker also sent along walking sticks turned from scrap airscrews for each pilot – a typical Fokker touch.

On 2 February *Jasta* Boelcke became part of the newly-formed JG III, commanded by Hptm Bruno Loerzer. All the component *Jagdstaffeln* were based in the vicinity of Courtrai. By mid-February a full complement of triplanes was probably on hand, but the unit retained some Albatros D V aircraft as well. Aces in Jasta B known to have flown triplanes include Paul Bäumer, Hermann Vallendor, Richard Plange, Karl Bolle, Hermann Frommherz, Karl Gallwitz and Otto Löffler.

One of the best of *Jasta* Boelcke's pilots in this era was Paul Bäumer, who was nearing his 24th birthday and came from Duisberg. Work as a pre-war dentist's assistant paid for his early flying lessons, and he gained his licence in the summer of 1914. Despite this, his early war service was with the infantry in both France and Russia, and after being wounded in the left arm, he transferred to the air service, passed through the usual two-seater period and was then finally accepted as a fighter pilot.

Bäumer's first fighter unit was *Jasta* 2, which he joined in the summer of 1917, before moving briefly to *Jasta* 5. Here, he scored three balloon victories, before returning to *Jasta* 2 (Boelcke) in August. By the end of the year he had scored 18 confirmed successes, making him the unit's highest-scoring surviving pilot. Bäumer's 19th to 22nd victories were all

The formidable commander of *Jasta* Boelcke, Oblt Karl Bolle, prepares himself for a flight in his Dr I (413/17) in May 1918. His personal insignia consisted of the fuselage bands, the central one of which was in yellow (the colour of his former unit, the *Kürassier-Regiment von Seydlitz Nr 7*), flanked by the black and white Prussian colours. The *Balkenkreuz* on the fuselage has been modified to proportions more in accordance with official instructions, and the white cross fields over-painted with a greenish wash. The upper wing crosses retained their earlier 'thick' style proportions, however. Note the Oigee telescopic sight mounted between the guns and the rack for flare cartridges below the cockpit sill. Bolle probably achieved his 7th to 12th victories whilst flying the triplane in April and May, and perhaps more. Note the early D VII in the background (*via VanWyngarden*)

A colourful display of *Jasta* Boelcke triplanes at Halluin-Ost in April 1918, the Dr Is being marked with the early style 'thick' *Balkenkreuz* – those on the wings would be retained, but the others were later changed to a more correct ratio. First in line is one of Fritz Kempf's highly decorated machines (perhaps 493/17), with Bolle's 413/17 third and Bäumer's 204/17 sixth. The reversed pattern *Jasta* B unit marking seen on the tails of the first two machines (black port, white starboard) may have been used as part of a system to identify the aircraft of two different *Ketten* (flights) within the *Staffel* (*via VanWyngarden*)

The *Jasta* B pilots of '*Kette* Kempf' pose with their walking sticks in front of a Dr I. These sticks had been turned from scrap propellers and presented to the men as gifts from Anthony Fokker himself. A *Kette* was generally a flight of three to six pilots within a *Jasta*, and the leader of this group was the veteran pilot Ltn Friedrich 'Fritz' Kempf (four victories). The pilot at the extreme left is unidentified, but the remainder are, from the left with their known victories, Ltns Wilhelm Papenmeyer (four – killed in action on 28 March 1918), Hermann Vallendor (six), Richard Plange (seven), Paul Schroder (one) and Kempf
(*HAC/UTD via VanWyngarden*)

scored in March 1918, during which time he was often flying Dr I 204/17, although he may have alternated with an Albatros D V. Photos supply proof that Bäumer also had a second Dr I (probably 209/17) marked with a red or yellow 'B' on the fuselage. According to Josef Jacobs, Bäumer enjoyed the manoeuvrability a rotary-engined aircraft provided, and found the Dr I perfectly suited to his style of close-in fighting.

His first claim in this machine came on 9 March, when he scrambled as part of a five-aircraft *Kette*. His combat report noted his black-white-red band on the fuselage of 204/17, and stated;

'1 km north of Zonnebeke, at 11.10 o'clock. I was flying with four other gentlemen from the *Staffel* to the Wytschaete bend, when we saw three single-seater flights of seven aircraft, each flying in formation to our front. We attacked the lower flight at a height of 2000 metres over Becelaere. First, I had a banking fight with a Sopwith from whom I had to break off again. Then I followed three Sopwith single-seaters from the same flight which were flying together.

'I attacked one of these at a height of 1500 metres, whereupon he flew towards me. After a short banking fight I, at a close distance, caused the

One of Germany's finest fighter pilots in his element – Paul Bäumer, seen seated in the cockpit of Dr I 204/17. This fine study reveals that the centre section struts were also painted black and white. As with Werner Voss and Josef Jacobs, Bäumer and the Dr I were a perfect match. He preferred the manoeuvrability of rotary-engined fighters over the speed of in-line-engined aircraft, and would achieve several victories with the triplane (*HAC/UTD via VanWyngarden*)

Sopwith to crash, the aircraft rearing up and then diving vertically down. I followed the falling opponent and saw him run vertically into the ground north of the Zonnebeke-Frezenberg Road. It was completely smashed up.'

It would appear that Bäumer's opponents were most likely Camels from No 65 Sqn, which reported an attack by Fokker triplanes, but which actually suffered no losses.

On 15 March the *Staffel* transferred to the 17th Army Front at Erchin, south-east of Douai, in preparation for the huge offensive

which would start six days later. Bäumer's best day came on 23 March, when he scored a triple. The first, his 20th victory (a No 46 Sqn Camel), was the *Jasta's* 200th kill of the war. There is substantial evidence to suggest that Bäumer was flying an Albatros D V on this particular flight. However, that afternoon at around 1515 hrs, he took off again, and this time he was almost certainly at the controls of one of his Dr Is. His second combat report of the day, sited north of Tilloy, is timed at 1545 hrs;

'I took off 15 minutes later than my *Staffel* because of a defective motor and flew in the direction of Arras. In the haze beneath me I suddenly sighted, at 800 metres, an enemy "working" aeroplane RE (8). I attacked the RE from out of the sun and placed myself under his tail. My opponent did not give me the chance to shoot at him, and attempted to escape in the direction of Arras. I kept behind him and shot at him from a short distance. The aeroplane ran, smoking, with its left wing into the ground and (was) completely smashed up.

'Then I flew, whilst being heavily shot at by flak, in a south-easterly direction and looked for my *Staffel*. Over Bapaume (at 1615 hrs) I sighted a second RE and attacked it at a height of 1000 metres. When he saw me, he banked toward me, shooting, upon which I flew under him and placed myself behind him. After a few shots, the opponent fell down burning. I saw the pieces of the wreck hit, still burning, to the north of

Bäumer also flew 209/17, which bore the standard *Jasta* B markings on the tail, but at the time this photograph was taken, its cowling was either all-black or factory finish solid olive. His personal marking consisted of a red (or yellow) 'B' on the fuselage sides just ahead of the cross, which was repeated on the top of the fuselage (*HAC/UTD via VanWyngarden*)

Despite the Sopwith Triplanes having been out of frontline service for some time, Fokker Dr Is were still occasionally being fired on by other German aircraft. In an effort to stop this from happening, some triplanes in both *Jasta* B and its sister unit in JG III, *Jasta* 36, were marked with additional national insignia on the tailplanes. Dr I 204/17, seen here, was the highly decorated aircraft of Vzfw Paul Bäumer, and it also bore crosses on thinly-applied white panels on each lower wing as well. Bäumer's machine also had a black border around its white rudder, which was a popular *Jasta* B touch. The cross on the starboard side of the rudder was also partially bordered in black when this photo was taken. Bäumer's main personal marking was a red-white-black diagonal band marked aft of the cockpit (*HAC/UTD via VanWyngarden*)

Bäumer is assisted with his Heinecke parachute harness prior to a flight in 204/17. The white rag knotted through a button hole in his coat was a common accessory among German pilots, and was used for wiping the goggles. Note the auxiliary undercarriage bracing seen on many *Jasta* Boelcke triplanes (*HAC/UTD via VanWyngarden*)

By early April 1918, the national insignia on triplanes of *Jasta* B were being modified to *Balkenkreuze* in accordance with the *Idflieg* directive of 17 March. This was first done in a manner which produced a 'thick' style of cross, as seen here on Vzfw Paul Bäumer's 204/17. In the case of this particular machine, the iron crosses on the top of the lower wing were now over-painted, and every wingtip was painted black, with a narrow white edge that was bordered by an even narrower red(?) strip on the lower two wings. This white/red border was also applied to the underside of the top wing, but not to the uppersurface. The white cross fields on the fuselage were generally reduced with a light greenish 'wash', as evidenced here, leaving a white border. The cross emblem on the tailplane was retained, but modified to *Balkenkreuz* form (*HAC/UTD via VanWyngarden*)

Beugnatre. No other German aeroplanes participated in this battle.'

The first RE 8 may have come from either Nos 5 or 59 Sqn, while the second one almost certainly was a No 59 Sqn aircraft – its wreckage was found three days later by advancing German troops.

After his stint on the Dr I, Bäumer became one of the few aces to fly the Pfalz D VIII, a rotary-engined biplane produced in small numbers – apparently he still preferred the agile qualities of a rotary-engined fighter. His successful combat record resulted in his promotion to reserve officer and, eventually, the *Pour le Mérite*. Injured in a crash on 29 May, Bäumer did not return to active duty until September, by which time *Jasta* Boelcke was equipped with Fokker D VIIs. He survived the war with 43 victories (more than any other pilot in the *Staffel*), only to die in a peacetime flying accident in 1927.

Leutnant der Reserve Hermann Vallendor was not quite 24 when he flew the Dr I with the Boelcke *Staffel*. From Offenberg in Baden, he had been an engineering student before the war, and like so many other fliers, began the conflict in the infantry. He rose from the ranks and was commissioned a Leutnant der Reserve on Christmas Eve 1915.

After becoming a pilot in 1916 Vallendor spent the first half of 1917 in *Fl Abt* 23, before going off to fighter school in June. He was sent to *Jasta* Boelcke in August 1917, although it was not until the beginning of February 1918 that he made his first kill. By March he was flying Dr I 195/17, marked with his white 'V' emblem on the fuselage sides and top, and on the centre section of the upper wing. Vallendor received credit for a victory on 27 March, and would bring his tally to five (some accounts say six) by the war's end. He had been awarded the Knight's Cross 2nd Class of the Zähringer Lion, with Swords, from his native state of Baden as well as the Iron Cross 1st Class.

Richard Plange came from Ellingson, and had celebrated his 25th birthday on Christmas Eve 1917. He had been wounded whilst

The stained and dirty white 'V' emblem on the side of 195/17 shows that Hermann Vallendor had been flying this Dr I for some time by early April 1918. The crosses on the fuselage and rudder are of the initial *Balkenkreuz* form applied to *Jasta* B aircraft. This machine evidences considerable signs of wear and oil stains, and the fuselage cross displays a smudged left arm. Also fitted was a tubular gun sight and the oft-seen auxiliary strut bracing. This particular Dr I was powered by a Rhemag-built Oberursel engine (*via VanWyngarden*)

serving with *Jasta* B in September, soon after joining this unit, but was back the following month. His first confirmed claim came in early November, and two more followed in early 1918. Plange scored three more kills in March, probably flying triplanes (his usual mount being 203/17), and his seventh came in April.

He moved to *Jasta* 36, within JG III, in May and became its *Staffelführer* on the 16th, but he was killed in action three days later during an attack upon a No 10 Sqn Armstrong-Whitworth FK 8 two-seater. Plange went down over Zillebeke in Dr I 546/17 and crashed inside Allied lines – the wreck was designated G 2/Bde/10.

Karl Bolle was born in June 1893 in Berlin, where his family owned a famous dairy. At the age of 19 he studied economics at Oxford University, where he was also something of an athlete in the ice hockey team. He credited his English education with teaching him the meaning of sportsmanship and fair play, but was not reluctant to return to Germany.

In 1913 Bolle reported to the Halberstadt contingent of the crack cavalry unit *Kürassier-Regiment von Seydlitz (Magdeburgisches) Nr 7* as a one-year volunteer. The war began before his enlistment was up, and he served with the regiment in France, Poland and Kurland, prior to joining the air service in early 1916. By July of that year he was flying two-seaters with *Kagohl* 4, and for a time his observer (prior to him taking pilot training) was none other than Lothar von Richthofen.

In October 1916, Bolle was flying with a different (unidentified) observer when they were attacked by five French single-seaters. In the ensuing engagement both crewmen were seriously wounded, but Bolle managed to bring his aircraft down just behind German lines and then drag his wounded observer to safety before he, too, collapsed.

After a period of hospitalisation and recuperation, Bolle returned to active duty with *Jasta* 28 in April 1917. As he had not yet fully recovered from his leg wound, his first duties there were as an adjutant. However, he eventually returned to the air and began learning the trade of a *Jadgflieger*. In this Bolle learned much from the superb example, and leadership, of two succeeding *Jasta* commanders, Ltn Karl-Emil Schaefer and Hptm Otto Hartmann. However, his best tutelage came from his friend, the formidable Bavarian ace Max Müller.

Bolle's study and hard work paid off, and by early 1918 he had achieved five victories. He then moved to *Jasta* Boelcke as its commander on 20 February 1918, just as the unit was really starting to make the most of its triplanes. Bolle resumed his scoring in April, usually flying Dr I 413/17 which he had decorated with the yellow colour of his old cavalry outfit, along with the black and white colours of Prussia. As part of JG III's move north to support the coming Kemmel Offensive, *Jasta* Boelcke had relocated to Halluin-Ost airfield by 17 April. Bolle continued to add to his tally during this time, and by the early summer had increased his score to more than a dozen.

Bolle's facility with the English language could come in handy in interrogating British prisoners, and he related the following episode in *Pour le Mérite Flieger* by Walter Zuerl (here translated by Jan Hayzlett);

'The English got into the habit of bombing Courtrai every day, and often, even several times a day. They were using the new de Havilland 9 biplane which was superior to our Fokker triplanes, particularly in its speed. One morning, one such squadron of nine aircraft on its return flight in the Ypres salient was pounced on by seven machines of my *Staffel* which, approaching the enemy at first from the side, had penetrated the squadron from the rear.

'I had targeted the leader's aircraft, which was flying in the middle and towards the front – however, during the *Staffel's* attack I had strayed a little forward. My opponent, who flew most skilfully, calmly allowed me to dive into the wedge of his formation and then had me completely surrounded before my comrades got there. The concentric fire from 18 machine guns covered my aeroplane so completely that I had to head for the ground with my fuel tank shot to pieces, my engine shot to pieces, and my machine pretty well ripped to shreds after having been able to give the leader's machine just one short burst.

'However, at the moment that I had started to go down in a spin, I thought I noticed that his aircraft was beginning to smoke. At this same time, the *Staffel* had engaged the English squadron in air combat. The *Staffel* landed smoothly a short time after I did (I had, in the meantime, counted a total of 42 bullet holes in my triplane).

'From the reports, it turned out that several of the English machines must have been heavily damaged – apart from the leader's aircraft, two more had been noticeably "marked", and another was said to have even burned for a moment. Enquiries amongst the ground observers did not give a clear picture – the air combat had, of course, been observed, and moreover, it had been seen that the machines under attack had put out a great deal of smoke. However, it could not be ascertained that they had crashed. So our efforts had apparently been in vain.

'A few days later, a lone DH 9 was shot down by flak south of Kemmel and its crew taken prisoner, unhurt. During their interrogation, they asked about a German triplane *Staffel*, which was widely feared and whose markings they described exactly. They also reported that several days earlier an English squadron, to which they belonged, had had quite a fight with these triplanes when on a return flight from Courtrai. The squadron's nine aircraft had in fact reached the lines, but five of the nine had been lost over their own territory as a result of emergency landings and crashes, and their crews were either dead or badly injured.

'So our efforts of a couple of days earlier had not been totally in vain, even if the enemy losses couldn't be included in the *Staffel's* tally of downed aircraft.'

It is difficult to match RAF combats with this action, but it seems fairly certain the DH 9s came from No 98 Sqn, and that the fight occurred on either 21 April, 3 May or 17 May 1918. Bolle would go on to achieve the lion's share of his 36 victories in the summer and autumn, flying the formidable D VII, and ended the war with the *Pour le Mérite*. He remained active in aviation in the 1920s and 30s, and was involved in the secret training of airmen for the new Luft-waffe. Bolle died in Berlin in 1955.

Hermann Frommherz was a little older than some of his comrades at 26, born in Waldshut on 10 August 1891. An engineering student, he was also an army reservist, and began the war in the infantry, being decorated for his bravery on the Russian Front. Transferring to the air service in June 1915, he also went to *Kagohl* 4, flying with *Kasta* 20, in February 1916. Whilst serving with the latter unit, Frommherz flew missions in the dangerous skies over Verdun and during the Somme offensive in 1916.

At the end of the year *Kasta* 20 was transferred to the Romanian Front and became part of *Kagohl* 1.

Frommherz flew further missions over Macedonia and Salonika, where his aggressiveness and sterling service resulted in his commission in the Reserves, and the award of the Knight's Cross of the Zähringer Lion with Swords 2nd Class. In March 1917 he returned to France and joined *Jasta* B, scoring his first two victories during 'Bloody April'. Frommherz was not victorious for some time afterwards, however, and over the winter of 1917-18 he was posted as an instructor to the flying school at Lübeck.

Frommherz did not return to the *Jasta* until May 1918, when he put in some time flying the Dr I in its final days with the unit. And although he had his own machine, it is not certain if either of his early June 1918 victories were claimed whilst flying it. He was posted to *Jasta* 27 in July as its new CO, and ended the war with 32 victories. Although Frommherz was nominated for the *Pour le Mérite*, the war ended before it was awarded – in some post-war photographs the veteran ace is shown wearing it, undoubtedly feeling he had earned it!

Ltn Karl Gallwitz was credited with shooting down Arthur Rhys Davids, the No 56 Sqn pilot who had downed Werner Voss. Gallwitz began his flying the usual way, via two-seaters in *Fl Abt (A)* 231. He was

Ltn Hermann Frommherz would score the majority of his 32 victories flying the Fokker D VII, although he may have achieved his 3rd and 4th successes (in early June) in a Dr I. Photographed shortly after returning from the Lübeck Flying School on 18 May, he is seen here posing in front of a Dr I with a black(?) and white sawtooth pattern painted onto its interplane struts. This machine was presumably his usual aircraft, and the strut painting an extension of the personal marking on the fuselage – a diamond band in black(?) and white. Note that the engine cowling was a solid colour, perhaps factory-finish olive, but more likely black (*via VanWyngarden*)

Karl Gallwitz (2nd from left) poses with his mechanics at Bavichove aerodrome, near Courtrai, in February 1918. This view clearly shows the black cowling and white face plate which was applied to most *Jasta* 2 Boelcke triplanes as part of their unit decor. This Dr I may have been 212/17 – note the leader's streamers affixed to both wingtip skids. Gallwitz attained a score of ten kills before being wounded in April, his last two claims (on 27 March and 21 April) being almost certainly achieved with the Dr I (*HAC/UTD via VanWyngarden*)

then posted to FA37 on the Russian Front, where he flew Roland D II fighters. He shot down two balloons with this unit in July 1917, then transferred to *Jasta* 29 in France, before moving just weeks later to *Jasta* B. By early 1918 Gallwitz had scored a total of eight victories, including Rhys Davids on 27 October 1917, and he scored two more whilst later flying the Dr I. Injured in a crash in April, he saw no further active duty.

Leutnant der Reserve Otto Löffler saw service in the *Grenadier Regiment König Friedrich Wilhelm Nr 10* prior to becoming a pilot. He was assigned to the Boelcke *Staffel* in the autumn of 1917, and claimed his first victory in early December. He flew several triplanes, including 190/17, in many actions in the spring of 1918, but did not score any further kills. Löffler was, however, twice shot down whilst flying the Dr I, and the last time he came down in 'No Man's Land' not far from the British trenches.

In the summer of 1918 Löffler's scoring increased dramatically, and by the end of October his tally had reached 15 – nearly all of these kills were obtained with BMW-engined Fokker D VIIs. Two decades later, Löffler's son would become a successful fighter ace in World War 2.

The *Staffel* marking employed on the triplanes of *Jasta* Boelcke consisted of a black/white tailplane, elevators and rear fuselage, with the colours being divided along the centreline of the fuselage. In some cases the starboard side of the fuselage was painted black and the port side white, but reversed examples of this pattern have also been seen in photographs – this may have served to divide the unit into two *Ketten*. Eventually, the engine cowlings also bore the Prussian black and white colours, displaying a white face plate on an otherwise black cowling. Photos indicate that this marking may have been preceded by an all-black cowling.

Jasta Boelcke's Ltn Otto Löffler (15 victories) poses with his Dr I 190/17. His personal marking was a fuselage band bordered by two white stripes. The band was probably lemon yellow, which was the colour of his old grenadier regiment. The triplane also displays typical '*Jasta* B' black and white decor. Löffler's second victory (a DH 4, claimed on 3 February) may have been achieved on the Dr I. However, the vast majority of his successes were scored whilst flying the BMW-engined Fokker DVII in late 1918
(*HAC/UTD via VanWyngarden*)

JASTA 4

Although *Jasta* 4 was part of JG I, it acquired its complement of triplanes somewhat belatedly. In anticipation of receiving the much-heralded Fokker D VII, the unit retained its Pfalz and Albatros biplanes well into April 1918 – with delivery of the D VII held up, *Jasta* 4 finally received the Dr I on the 20th of that month. Later, the unit received some ex-*Jasta* 6 and 11 triplanes when those units obtained D VIIs in May.

The first example of the Dr I to be lost in combat by the unit was 546/17, which was shot down near Corbie on 16 May with two-victory pilot Ltn Fedor Hübner at the controls. The German was taken prisoner, and his demise credited to Camels of JG I's old opponents, No 209 Sqn.

Jasta 4 was in fact the last *Staffel* of the *Geschwader* to fly the triplane, operating the type well into June. The *Staffel* usually identified its Dr Is with an off-white colour (very likely pale blue) applied to the cowlings, struts, wheel covers and, in some cases, the tailplane. Pilots of the unit did

Jasta 4 became the last of three JG I Staffeln to be equipped with the Dr I (Jasta 10 never operated the type in quantity) by 20 April 1918. In May the Jasta received more triplanes from Jasta 6 and 11, as those units had by then begun re-equipping with Fokker D VIIs. Here, Jasta 4 commander Ltn Ernst Udet poses by the wing of his Dr I (586/17) at Beugneux-Cramoiselle in June, this aircraft having previously been flown by Ltn Hans Kirschstein of Jasta 6. The fighter retains its earlier colour scheme of diagonal black and white stripes over much of its surfaces, although the crosses on the underside of the lower wings have been changed from their initial fully-bordered form following the 13 May directive. In the background is another Jasta 4 Dr I, bearing the very light (almost certainly sky-blue) cowling, struts and wheel covers which characterised many other triplanes from that unit. The other pilots in this photograph are, from left to right, Ltns Julius Bender, Egon Koepsch, Karl Meyer and Heinrich Drekmann (via VanWyngarden)

quite well with their ageing Dr Is during the Marne Offensive (which began on 27 May), when JG I faced the French instead of its traditional British foes. By July the Staffel had replaced its triplanes with D VIIs.

On 20 May a new Staffelführer was appointed – Ltn Ernst Udet, recently returned from a leave in Munich, where he had been recuperating from a severe ear infection. Whilst at home, Udet had received the news that his long-awaited Pour le Mérite had been awarded – news that thrilled his fiancée Eleonore 'Lo' Zink even more than it did him. Now he was eager to resume his scoring streak.

Unlike his former leader von Richthofen, Udet loved to fly. He had a passion for all things mechanical, especially aeroplanes and motorcycles. Neither the 'soldier through and through' nor the marksman Richthofen was, Udet was a gifted natural pilot, caricaturist and a gregarious raconteur. Carl Zuckmayer, an artillerist visiting JG I, later recalled;

'. . . (I first) met there a short, restless, wiry, ebullient and unusually humorous, often extremely witty, flying leutnant who had been honoured with the Pour le Mérite – Ernst Udet. We hit it off together after our first few words.'

One of Udet's triplanes at Jasta 4 was Dr I 586/17 – formerly the machine of Hans Kirschstein of Jasta 6 (see below). This machine still

Udet's last triplane with *Jasta* 4 was seemingly 593/17, marked with a small *LO!* emblem in a square, which was either chalked or painted on in white. This was a 'thumbnail' sketch for the *Staffel* 'artist' to use as he applied a larger version to the fuselage just aft of the smaller one, although in this instance it was apparently never completed, except in chalk outline. This Dr I also bore a white chevron on its factory-finish tailplane, with national insignia in the ultimate format described in the 13 May order (*via VanWyngarden*)

Left
Udet's striped 586/17 is seen at the captured French airfield at Beugneux in June-July 1918, with the burnt French hangars visible in the background. The white fuselage stripes are considerably oil-stained and weathered compared with the fresher white of the cross outline – wheel covers may also have been black/white too. Just visible on the fuselage above the bottom wing are portions of Udet's *LO!* insignia, probably painted in red to contrast with the striping. The cowling retains its earlier *Jasta* 6 black finish, and note the striped interplane struts and the rectangular access panel just ahead of the air intake – both characteristic features of Dr Is from *Jasta* 6 (*HAC/UTD via VanWyngarden*)

bore the dazzling black and white stripes of its former pilot, and Udet did little to change the colour scheme except to add his usual *LO!* insignia to the fuselage, probably in red. At some point in late June the engine of this Dr I lost a cylinder in flight, tearing off the cowling and further damaging the aircraft – Udet was fortunate to make a successful emergency landing.

He also flew Dr I 593/17, which seems to have borne a factory finish, with *LO!* chalked or painted on the fuselage side, and a white chevron on the camouflaged tailplane. Udet and his pilots flew their triplanes from Beugneux-Cramoiselle airfield throughout June, and the ace had some memorable encounters with French aeroplanes, as he wrote in *Kreuz wider Kokarde*;

'Because French fliers developed very little offensive spirit, (we made) our combat flights far behind the enemy line . . . in the evenings because then we had the sun at our backs and with this, good possibilities to attack. So one evening we six were flying along, and found ourselves at 4000 metres and not fired at by flak because it was very hazy. A flight of four SPAD single-seaters made a shy attempt to block our way, but after one of them was shot at by one of my gentlemen, they preferred to break off from us and went in a glide down to their airfield.

'We flew on, and a bit later I noticed far below us three aircraft coming from our front. We went down after them in a dive, and very soon recognised them as Bréguet two-seaters, which were apparently coming home after artillery spotting, and had not thought they would be attacked by the "Boches" in the next second, just over their captive balloons. Two, however, realised the situation, and at the last moment . . . took their leave by diving below. The third one, however, appeared to be more courageous and took on my attack.

'He turned toward me, but I caught up to him very fast and now hung directly under his tail. After a well-aimed burst, the aircraft made a turn to the right, downwards and flew right under me. I immediately followed and observed that the pilot, head laying backwards, was sitting in his seat while the observer lay stretched out on the floor of his cockpit. So both were dead, but despite this their barge flew on, now to the left, now to the right, exactly as the wind blew, slowly going lower all the time.

'Now I attempted to set the entire thing on fire . . . (after) 200 shots from an extremely close distance I was successful. The Bréguet, with its dead occupants, began to burn under its fuselage while still flying south. Gradually the fire got the upper hand, and at 4000 metres the aircraft broke apart with a great flame, the charred pieces falling downwards.'

JASTA 5

This unit does not feature too often in the triplane story, despite it briefly being completely equipped with the type at Cappy in early May. These

65

In May 1918 *Jasta 5* was based at Cappy, where it received enough cast-off Dr Is from JG I to fully equip the unit. One was 139/17 from *Jasta 11*, which was occasionally flown by Offz Stv Josef Mai, who attained his 12th victory (a BF 2b) in this aircraft on 15 May. This particular Dr I probably retained its red colouration on the cowling, wheel covers and undercarriage struts. A light-coloured disc marking which had been applied in the previous unit seems to have been painted over with solid olive, and an additional white(?) vertical band applied. The dirty white horizontal fuselage stripe was also a remnant of the machine's former owner, but the tail section was probably painted *Jasta 5* green. Mai achieved kills in 554/17 and 592/17 (*via VanWyngarden*)

aircraft again came from *Jastas* 6 and 11, as those *Staffeln* had by then re-equipped with the D VII. NCO pilot Josef Mai was one of the unit's top aces, and he achieved three of his thirty victories flying triplanes.

According to the research of the late German historian Dr Gustav Bock, Mai's 12th victory (a Bristol Fighter of No 11 Sqn) was achieved on 15 May in Dr I 139/17. Five days later, flying Dr I 554/17, he was credited with a Camel, which was only confirmed some weeks later as his 14th victory. In the meantime, Mai had flamed another Camel (of No 65 Sqn) in Dr I 592/17 on 2 June, which was credited as his 13th victory.

Josef Mai was no youngster, having been born in 1887. On 27 September 1918 he was finally promoted to leutnant der reserve, and like several others, he was proposed for the 'Blue Max' but never received it due to the armistice. Mai survived the war and finally died in 1982, aged 94.

The Dr Is were used by *Jasta* 5 only until it could obtain D VIIs, and most had been replaced by July 1918. Many of the unit's triplanes continued to carry the markings of their previous owners, and any that were re-painted were probably done on the whim of the individual pilots.

JASTA 6

Another *Staffel* of the elite JG I, *Jasta* 6 could boast several aces who gained victories flying the triplane in 1918, among them Franz Hemer, Johann Janzen, Wilhelm Reinhard and Hans Kirschstein. The unit was equipped with Dr Is from February until May, by which time the first examples of the D VII had arrived. The *Staffel's* triplanes bore the unit's traditional marking of chord-wise black and white zebra stripes on the horizontal tail surfaces, and black cowlings.

Following the advances made in the Great March Offensive, JG I occupied Léchelle airfield on the 26th, where this colourful line-up of *Jasta 6* triplanes was photographed. National markings were in the midst of being changed to *Balkenkreuz* form, as mandated on 17 March, and a variety of crosses are visible. On the far right is Ltn Franz Hemer's machine (possibly 595/17), which displays part of his light-coloured wavy-line emblem. Next is Ltn Robert Tüxen's machine, with a black-bordered white band which was either thinly applied or considerably dirtied. The fourth triplane – apparently 556/17 – is thought to have been previously flown by Ltn Ludwig 'Lutz' Beckmann (who transferred to *Jasta* 56 on 11 March). If so, it may have borne a white wavy line on a red vertical band – red and white were the colours of Beckmann's native Westphalia. This band was applied over a previous marking of a white lightning bolt (*HAC/UTD via VanWyngarden*)

Still wearing his parachute harness and flying togs, Vzfw Franz Hemer inspects battle damage to the wing of his distinctively-marked Dr I (595/17?). Hemer was nicknamed 'Locken' by his comrades due to his curly blonde hair, and the light wavy fuselage line referred to this. Late in life Hemer recalled that the line was yellow, and if so, then it was a very light yellow, or possibly white. Hemer may have scored most or all of his 3rd to 10th victories (out of a final tally of 18) in March to May 1918 flying the Dr I (*Frau Margot Hemer via VanWyngarden*)

Vzfw Franz Hemer had gained frontline flying experience in *Fl Abt (A)* 283 prior to joining *Jastaschule* I. Arriving at *Jasta* 6 in September 1917, he had scored twice before the new year, and would claim four or five more in March and April with the Dr I, including, apparently, 595/17.

Hemer's nickname of 'Locken' stemmed from his blond wavy hair, and his triplanes were marked with a white (or perhaps very pale yellow) wavy line in reference to this. Hemer is also reported to have used a *'brennschere'* (curling iron) as a personal insignia on a different aircraft! By the end of the war he had scored 18 victories overall, and lived until 1982.

Johann Janzen from West Prussia gained his eighth victory the day before his 24th birthday. He first saw action with the army, being commissioned in the field prior to moving into flying. Janzen had served with *Kasta* 12 and *Kagohl* 2 prior to joining *Jasta* 23 in November 1916, and he scored one victory with the unit the following February.

He was then transferred to *Jasta* 6 in October, and by late 1917 had increased his score to three. Janzen began flying triplanes (including 403/17) the following spring, downing an RE 8 on 27 March for victory number four – the next day he was given command of *Jasta* 4, still within JG I. He later moved back to *Jasta* 6 as CO on 28 April, following Wilhelm Reinhard's appointment as leader of JG I.

On 9 May JG I's regular antagonists, the Camels of No 209 Sqn, shot him down (his victor was Capt O C LeBoutillier), although Janzen survived unhurt. His was a lucky escape, for a bullet had severed the rudder control cables of his triplane, causing him to fall to the ground completely out of control. A strong wind blew his machine into German territory, and it hit soft marshland near the River Somme. Although understandably shaken by the crash, Janzen was up in another triplane again just two days later.

Dr I 403/17 forms the backdrop for *Jasta* 6's Ltn Johann Janzen, a successful ace who rose to command the unit on 28 April. His personal emblem was a white wavy 'snakeline' on a black band, which probably encircled the fuselage, and had a narrow white border on its forward edge. The white rudder was painted over with solid olive or black to produce a five-centimetre white border. There also appears to be some form of 'eye' marking on the front cowling panel (*via VanWyngarden*)

Through May and early June he ran his score up to 13, with perhaps all of his last ten kills being claimed in Dr Is. However, he was brought down over French territory in one of the new Fokker D VIIs on 9 June, Janzen having in fact shot himself down due to the malfunction of his interrupter gear – he shot off his own propeller as soon as he opened up on a SPAD.

Oblt Wilhelm 'Willi' Reinhard hailed from Düsseldorf, where he

had been born in March 1891. A Regular army officer, he had joined the *Badisches Fussartillerie-Regiment Nr 14* in 1909 and been severely wounded in November 1914. He duly returned to the front seven months later, but then transferred into the air service. Wounded again, Reinhard was back in early 1916, still flying two-seaters firstly in France and then in the Balkans.

He became a fighter pilot in 1917, joining *Jasta* 11 in June, but was wounded in September after scoring six victories. Reinhard returned to the *Geschwader* to take command of *Jasta* 6 in November, and he scored several more kills in early 1918 – a number of these flying the Dr I.

Promoted to hauptmann on 22 March, and with 12 credited claims to his name, Reinhard then took command of JG I following the loss of Manfred von Richthofen on 21 April, and by mid-June his score had risen to 20. He was nominated for the *Pour le Mérite* but was killed testing a new fighter design at the aircraft trials at Adlershof on 3 July, so this prestigious medal was not awarded (it was not given posthumously, even if the proposed recipient had been nominated prior to his death).

Hans Kirschstein, from Koblenz, was 21 when he began flying the Dr I. He had already seen war service in Poland and France with the sapper outfit *3.Pionier-Bataillon 'von Rauch'*, and whilst serving in Galicia in 1915 he contracted malaria. Kirschstein duly returned to his homeland, and upon recovery was sent back to the Western Front, prior to transferring to the air service in May 1917.

After becoming a pilot, he subsequently served with several two-seater *Abteilungen*, and even participated in a bombing raid on Dover on one occasion. Kirschstein eventually volunteered for fighters, and on 13 March 1918 he joined *Jasta* 6 – he would eventually become the unit's most successful pilot. During his first week flying fighters he downed a Camel of No 54 Sqn, and by April his tally stood at six. Kirschstein more than doubled this during May, with his 16th kill falling on the 30th, and in June he enjoyed further success when he increased his score to 27. Richard Wenzl, who had transferred to *Jasta* 6 on 15 May, wrote;

'Kirschstein then came back from leave and took up his tasks in the old spirit, shooting one down almost every day even when there was almost nothing happening (as far as enemy air activity was concerned).He had

Wilhelm 'Willi' Reinhard, commander of *Jasta* 6, stands by his crash-landed Dr I in his *Flieger-kombination* (flying suit), holding his Heinecke parachute harness, in mid-March 1918. The black and white tailplane striping which identified *Jasta* 6 aircraft is shown to good advantage, along with the black cowling. What is left of the rudder is also black. Reinhard lost his upper wing fabric in flight, which in turn led to structural failure. He succeeded in keeping enough control to force-land, however, although the Dr I flipped over when its wheels touched the ground, causing most of the damage visible in this photograph. Reinhard's star was on the rise at this period, and he was promoted to hauptmann on 22 March. His score had reached 12 by mid-April, and he subsequently took command of JG I following von Richthofen's death (*P Kilduff via VanWyngarden*)

just gotten the hang of it, and was recognised as the only one who might truly emulate Richthofen. He painted his aeroplane in black and white diagonal lines. He claimed that this made aiming more difficult for his opponent, and that is why he also called the crate "the optical illusion".'

Kirschstein flew both 586/17 and his succeeding D VII decorated in this 'dazzle-painted' manner.

He was awarded the *Pour le Mérite* on the date of his last victory (24 June), having taken acting command of the *Jasta* on 10 June following the loss of Johann Janzen. However, Kirschstein was himself killed in a crash on 16 July, flying as a passenger in a two-seat Hannover CL II flown by another *Jasta* 6 pilot, Ltn Markgraf. The latter had been sent to collect him from an aircraft park at Fismes, where the ace's Fokker was being overhauled. It was later established that the novice Markgraf had never flown a Hannover before.

Of all his kills, Kirschstein's second victory was perhaps his most notable as far as his opponents were concerned. Flying his Dr I, he had downed an Armstrong-Whitworth FK 8 of No 2 Sqn on 17 March, the aircraft's demise resulting in the award of the Victoria Cross for its Canadian pilot, 2Lt A A McLeod.

Kirschstein's fire had set the two-seater ablaze, the damage and flames being so great that the observer, Lt A W Hammond MC, had been forced to climb onto the top of the fuselage. McLeod too had to vacate his cockpit, standing on the left lower wing-root while he held onto the smouldering control column in order to glide down crab-like so as to keep the flames away from himself and Hammond. They eventually crashed between the trenches.

Despite wounds and burns, McLeod pulled his unconscious observer from the wreck and dragged him a safe distance away from the aircraft, which had crashed with its bombload still aboard – both men were later rescued by South African troops. Sadly, although McLeod survived his ordeal, he was to die in the great influenza epidemic in Canada two days prior to the Armistice.

JASTA 7 AND JOSEF JACOBS

The tale of the triplane in *Jasta* 7 is a unique one, as it revolves around a lone, and singularly successful, pilot – *Staffelführer*, Leutnant der Reserve Josef Carl Jacobs. This fascinating personality would finish the war with over 40 confirmed claims (various sources credit Jacobs with scores varying from 41 to 48 – he himself claimed 47 in his later years).

What is certainly clear is that Jacobs flew the Dr I far longer operationally than any other ace. Yet, he is the least known of the three most famous exponents of the triplane, after Manfred von Richthofen and Werner Voss. His outstanding accomplishments deserve better notoriety.

Jacobs was a Rhinelander, born on 15 May 1894. He had started flying lessons at the age of 18, and as soon as the war began he volunteered for

Jasta 6's Ltn Hans Kirschstein flew this flamboyantly decorated triplane (586/17). This rare photograph comes from the album of Franz Hemer, and was originally captioned, 'Lt Kirschstein mit seinem Monteuren' (Lt Kirschstein with his Mechanics). *Jasta* 6 comrade Richard Wenzl described the markings of Kirschstein's Fokker D VII and previous Dr I in his book *Richthofen Flieger*;

'He painted his machine in black and white diagonal lines. He maintained that this made it more difficult for the enemy to aim at. Therefore, he also called his crate "the optical illusion".'

It is obvious from this picture that the white paint at least was thinly-applied, and somewhat translucent, for it appears darker than the freshly-applied white border of the cross on the fuselage. Both surfaces of the top wing were decorated, as were the interplane struts. It seems evident from this view that the diagonal stripes on the fuselage ended at a vertical demarcation line at about mid-cockpit, a detail not generally evident in the views of this machine after it went to *Jasta* 4, where it was taken over by Ernst Udet, who added his *LO!* emblem (*Frau Margot Hemer via VanWyngarden*)

69

Josef Jacobs (second from left) had at least two black triplanes available to him at *Jasta* 7 – 450/17 and 470/17 (he told an interviewer in 1974 that he once had three, although nothing survives to confirm this). This particular machine is thought to be 470/17, which his combat reports of 15 and 21 September describe as black, with black/white-outlined crosses on both sides of the fuselage behind the pilot's seat, and a white rudder. The white cross borders on the fuselage cross are indistinct probably due to oil staining or other weathering
(*HAC/UTD via VanWyngarden*)

the *Fliegertruppe.* The future ace began his service as a pilot in *Feldflieger Abteilung* 11 in July 1915, where he flew a variety of LVG, Albatros and Aviatik B- and C-types (two-seaters). On several occasions during this period he and his observers tangled inconclusively with French aircraft.

In December of that year Jacobs had his first flight in a Fokker *Eindecker,* and two months later his sterling service resulted in his promotion to leutnant der reserve. On 21 March 1916, the *Eindeckers* of *FFl Abt* 11 were grouped with those of two other units into *Fokkerstaffel West,* and Jacobs duly claimed both his and the unit's first victory on 12 May when he downed a Caudron.

This unit formed the basis of *Jasta* 12 that autumn, but not long after it was created, Jacobs, with one confirmed and two unconfirmed claims, moved to *Jasta* 22 following a stint as an instructor at *Jastaschule* I. Whilst with his new unit Jacobs flew Albatros D II 1072/16, emblazoned with his nickname *Köbes* on the fuselage sides. Further victories came frustratingly slowly, although he was gaining valuable experience, and in August 1917 he was given command of *Jasta* 7 on the Flanders Front. There, he proved a very potent *Staffel* leader, increasing his score to 12 whilst flying Albatros and Pfalz D types.

On 27 February 1918 Jacobs went to the 4th Army Air Park at Ghent to pick up his *'new triplane'* – this was probably 450/17, which he would fly on many combat missions for the next eight months. He would also acquire a second Dr I (470/17), and had both aircraft painted entirely in the *Staffel's* black identification colour.

In his elderly years, Jacobs told an interviewer that at one time he had *three* triplanes, but there is no documentary or photographic evidence to confirm this. These were the only ones in the *Jasta,* for the remaining pilots all flew Albatros and Pfalz fighters, and later the Fokker D VII.

It was always useful for men to quickly identify their leader when in the air, and conveniently a lone triplane amidst a pack of biplanes always stood out. There is circumstantial evidence from RAF reports of encounters with *two* triplanes from *Jasta* 7, which indicates that Jacobs may have occasionally allowed one of his best pilots to also fly a Dr I as well. Indeed, Carl Degelow claimed in his memoirs that he flew the triplane whilst serving in *Jasta* 7, prior to becoming the commander of *Jasta* 40.

It is clear that Jacobs himself alternated between flying his triplanes and his Pfalz D IIIa or Albatros D V, and later D VII, choosing to fly his Dr I when he was on low-level missions such as balloon attacks, or when there was a low cloud ceiling. As he later stated, by mid-1918 it was impossible to climb above the British patrols, and he preferred to fly low with his Dr I and let his opponents come down to him. The triplane was much better

This unique photo shows Josef Jacobs' Dr I 450/17 of *Jasta* 7 in its most famous configuration. His combat report for his two balloon victories on 14 May 1918 describes the colour scheme as, 'black triplane with a devil's head on both sides of the fuselage behind the pilot's seat'. As this photograph shows, most of the lower portion of the devil's 'wing' was white, with an apparently red upper portion, white lips and horns and golden-yellow hair and beard. Even at this late date, the crosses on the upper surface of the bottom wing were deemed necessary by Jacobs to prevent over-eager German pilots from mistaking his aircraft for a Sopwith Triplane, or some 'new' Allied type (*via VanWyngarden*)

This line-up of *Jasta* 7's black fighters poses something of an enigma. The two triplanes closest to the camera are clearly Jacobs', (the second is probably 470/17), but the extreme left one with white crosses does not match any available description, and hardly seems to be 470/17. Nor does it seem likely it is 450/17 with the devil emblem over-painted. Perhaps 450/17 is out of the picture and the Dr I with white crosses was the third triplane Jacobs mentioned in later years? The fifth aircraft in the line up is a Fokker D VII, which bears Jacobs' devil's head emblem (*via VanWyngarden*)

close to the ground, and if the weather forced British machines to fly at lower altitudes, then Jacobs in his triplane was able to hold a distinct advantage.

He at first experienced some disappointment with the Dr I, his diary recording on 24 March 1918, '. . . a third flight with my triplane. It is much slower than the Albatros D V, and therefore not very useful. At low altitudes it is very manoeuvrable and equal to the English (aircraft)'. However, his opinion soon improved, although (like Richard Wenzl) he had trouble adjusting to the type's instability as a gun platform;

'3 April 1918 – at altitudes up to 2000 metres the triplane is better than the Albatros and Pfalz, and much more manoeuvrable, but you have to test fly her for long periods in order to familiarise (yourself), for she's very unstable when shooting.'

Jacobs grew to appreciate the type, and his black triplane soon left a vivid impression on his opponents. On 12 April 1918 he got into a scrap with SE 5s from No 74 Sqn, enjoying a turning battle ('*Kurvenkampf*') with Lt J I T 'Taffy' Jones. Jacobs' opponent was on his first patrol as a fighter pilot, although he would quickly gain over 30 victories by the summer. Jones only survived the encounter because he had remembered what his flight commander, Mick Mannock, had told him;

'Don't ever try to dogfight a triplane on anything like equal terms as regards height, otherwise he will get on your tail and stay there until he shoots you down.'

Jones later wrote nearly identical descriptions of this combat in all three of his post-war books (in the inter-war years he came to mistakenly believe his opponent had been Eduard von Schleich), in one case even accurately stating that the enemy pilot 'had a small, square face, and a puggish little nose'. His account as told in his 1934 Mannock biography *King of Air Fighters* is worth quoting;

'Two miles away and about 2000 ft above, I spotted a large flight of biplanes, led by a triplane, heading straight for us. The enemy leader soon took advantage of the gap between my flight and I, and brought his formation into it . . . and soon he was on my tail, firing sweet bullets of welcome to No 74 Sqn. Wisely I kept my head, and immediately put my machine into a steep bank, held the stick tight into my stomach, kept my throttle wide open and prayed hard – the gentleman who was doing his best to kill me was an old hand at this game.

'A sure sign of an old hand is that he reserves his ammunition and only fires in short bursts. This Hun on my tail was so close I could easily discern his features. His machine was painted black, with a white band (sic) around the fuselage just behind the cockpit, and he was flying it superbly. It seemed to slither around after me . . . as soon as I saw him commence to zoom up to change his position I obeyed Mick's instructions and put on full bottom rudder and my machine did a turn of a spin. I went for home, kicking my rudder from side to side to make the shooting more difficult for the enemy.

'It was a joy to see my little SE 5 gaining ground on the triplane and the Pfalz, and to listen to the fading rattle of the staccato barking of the enemy's guns as my machine gradually outstripped her opponents.'

Jacobs abandoned the chase, and later on the same flight briefly attacked some Bristol Fighters, and 'then flak scored a hit on my propeller', but he made it safely back.

Jacobs made his first claim with a triplane on 11 April, and many more would follow. On 14 May (one day before his 24th birthday) he flamed two French kite balloons in his Dr I. His combat report for that day contains the first available description of its now-famous colour scheme;

'Fok. Dr I 450/17: black triplane with a devil's head on both sides of the fuselage behind the pilot's seat.

'At 0410 hrs I started with my *Staffel* for a patrol to the front – because there was little aerial activity, and I noticed some English balloons through the clouds, I decided for a balloon attack. With my whole *Staffel* I raced down through the clouds, immediately opening fire at the first which ignited at once, burning fiercely. Then I opened fire at a second while a Pfalz (Uffz Mertens) at the same time fired at a third one. Both immediately burst into flames. I could only fire for a moment at the third balloon because I was fiercely fired at from the ground by MGs and small guns. The last balloon was very quickly hauled in, and about 8-10 observers jumped from all of them. All *Staffel* machines landed safely at their base.'

It is thought that Jacobs continued to fly Dr I 450/17 with the red and white devil's head emblem well into October – in interviews in the 1970s, Jacobs once referred to the insignia as a 'fire-spitting witch', and another time as 'the god of the north wind', but several contemporary combat reports simply call it a devil's head. It was an ironic choice of emblem, as Jacobs was a devoutly religious young man who attended church frequently, and who never flew without a small leather pouch containing several holy medals.

His combat reports describe his other machine (470/17) as a 'Black aircraft with black crosses surrounded with white on both sides of the fuselage behind the pilot's seat. White rudder', and several photos seem to feature this machine. Curiously, a single photograph of a *Jasta* 7 line-up at Ste Marguerite taken late in the war shows two black triplanes, one of which is marked with white crosses on the fuselage and wings. The serial number of this white-crossed machine is unknown – it may be either 450 or 470/17 overpainted (which seems unlikely), or perhaps it was the *third* triplane Jacobs mentioned in the 1970s?

What is certain is that Jacobs found the Oberursel engines of his triplanes wearing out as time wore on, and replacements were becoming more and more difficult to come by. He neatly solved this problem by

Jasta 7's Staffelführer Josef Jacobs is seen here in full flying kit, sat on the cockpit sill of one of his all-black triplanes. Although he would occasionally fly an Albatros or Pfalz D IIIa, and later a Fokker D VII, Jacobs continually flew missions in the Dr I from March 1918 until the final weeks of the war, scoring in the region of 30 victories with the type. He was undoubtedly the supreme Fokker Dr I ace in terms of the number of victories he claimed (HAC/UTD via VanWyngarden)

Josef Jacobs poses with his pilots. They are, from left to right, Uffz Peisker (one victory), Uffz Paul Hüttenrauch (eight), Uffz August Eigenbrodgt (three), Uffz Sicho (on wing), Ltn Willi Negben (four), Jacobs, Ltn Bannenberg, Uffz Jupp Böhne (on wing), Ltn Wirth, Ltn Rath(?) and unidentified (*HAC/UTD via VanWyngarden*)

making a standing offer to the German frontline troops in his vicinity – if they brought in a rotary engine from a downed Allied machine in good condition, he would give them a case of champagne. As he later chuckled, 'I never lacked for engines after that'.

It is apparent that both 450 and 470/17 eventually flew with captured 130 hp Clerget engines and British propellers, which overcame the triplane's speed handicap somewhat, and rendered both machines formidable weapons. Jacobs' diary entry for 19 July tells of a typical combat during the furious summer days over Flanders;

'I left with my *Kette* for the front, where I saw through the light haze two-seaters and single-seaters coming from Bailleul just below the clouds at an altitude of hardly more than 1500 metres, being fired at by German flak. My red warning flare had just been fired when a flight of SEs came out of the clouds firing furiously at me. Right away I turned toward one SE, but was then attacked from behind by three of them. At the same time I also saw three Bristol Fighters shooting as they passed me, so I dived. In the meantime, a second SE formation came to their assistance, as did two German *Jastas*. All engaged in the whirlwind battle.

'One moment I held this enemy in sight, and the next moment shook that enemy (from my sights) without being able to shoot properly myself. Suddenly I watched another opponent going after a Fokker. I fired, and the Englishman gave up. A second one came to his aid, and I quickly had him "wrapped up" and did not let him loose.

'I followed 50 metres behind him, and when he wanted to straighten out I shot him full of holes so that he turned toward Germany and prepared to land. He glided very slowly across a road, pulled his aeroplane up a little and then it turned over on its head. He immediately jumped out and ran into a deserted trench, followed by some soldiers.

'When I came home I at once took my car and drove to the landing site. It was a brand new SE 5a with an American 1st Lieutenant as pilot. His name was A M Roberts (of No 74 Sqn). He had been at the front for three months, and was astonished at the speed of my triplane. As a person he was very nice. He much regretted the death of Richthofen. He gave me his zippered map case.'

The black triplanes of Jacobs were becoming well-known on the Flanders Front, and by 21 July, with his official tally at 23, he finally won the long-awaited *Pour le Mérite* and a well-deserved leave followed.

It is interesting to note that his name and accomplishments were not unknown to his RAF opponents. The diary of No 56 Sqn pilot Capt O C Holleran, another 'Yank in the RAF', noted on 13 August that on a misty morning patrol, '. . . Jacobs, in a silver triplane, flew for miles just under me'.

Of course, Jacobs was on leave at this time and he never flew a silver Dr I, but it is noteworthy that Holleran apparently knew that Jacobs generally flew a triplane (perhaps another *Jasta* 7 pilot was flying one of his commander's machines, which might have looked silvery in the dim morning light?). Six days later, Holleran wrote;

'It is a certainty that war (an offensive) is going to break out of this front. We have nothing official, but I recognised both Richthofen's and Jacobs' squadrons among that mob this morning, and they are Fritz's super people.'

It seems the successes of *Jasta* 7 under Jacobs' leadership were earning the unit a reputation as well.

Jacobs returned from leave on 24 August, but did not score again until he got an RE 8 on 13 September, then victories followed one after another in rapid succession. Counting the RE 8, in the next five weeks he added 19 aircraft and four balloons to take his tally to 47. And although his diary stops at 26 September, Jacobs experienced a memorable action on 3 October which he often recounted to interviewers post-war.

He awoke to the sounds of machine guns and Hispano-Suiza engines, as a British fighter squadron launched an early-morning attack on his airfield. Quickly slipping his *Fliegerkombination* on over his pyjamas, Jacobs dashed out to his triplane, which was being prepared by his mechanics. In a few seconds he had climbed into the cockpit, buckled his parachute onto his harness, adjusted the safety belt and was taking off.

Almost immediately he was on the tail of an SE 5a (as he remembered), with his guns banging away. He lost this opponent in the clouds and smoke, but had brought it down. Soon he was firing at another SE when there was a sudden smash on the nose of his Dr I – so violent he thought he might have shot off his own airscrew. The triplane fell out of control, crashed and cartwheeled – Jacobs was thrown out of the aircraft, but fortunately (as he enjoyed relating) he landed on a manure pile, which cushioned his landing!

With his head throbbing, he saw that 'my dear black triplane that had been a part of me in so many struggles was now no more'. All the RAF aircraft had disappeared by then, and as he heard the grumbling of a BMW engine he looked up to see his comrade 'Jupp' Böhne flying overhead in his D VII to check on his CO. Though Jacobs recalled his antagonists as SEs, the 'official' record gives him credit for two Camels on that day.

It is believed that the Dr I lost that day was 470/17. Surviving combat reports filed by Jacobs on the 8th, 9th, 15th and 19th of October all describe the devil's head marking on a black triplane, and thus it is assumed that 450/17 was still operational. It is unlikely such an elaborate marking would have been re-painted on a different aircraft at this desperate stage of the war, given the severe supply shortage in the German army.

On 14 October, American Lt Kenneth Unger of No 210 Sqn was in a fight with an all-black Fokker triplane, claiming it down 'out of control'. No 210 Sqn had frequently mixed it up with *Jasta* 7 on previous occasions, and Unger was no novice, ending the war as a 14-victory ace with the DFC. However, he clearly he did not manage to finish off the black triplane, which must have been flown by Jacobs.

Given the incomplete status of available records, it is difficult to be precise in the matter of what aircraft Jacobs achieved which particular victories in. However, in his final score of at least 47 or 48 claimed since early 1916, it is likely that more than half (perhaps as many as 30) were achieved in his Fokker triplanes. This without question makes him the leading Fokker Dr I ace of the war.

After the Great War ended Jacobs fought against the communists with the *Freikorps* in Kurland in 1919, before becoming a flying instructor with the Turkish air force. Later still he went into the aviation business, and also became an avid sportsman, achieving success in bobsledding, motorcar and speedboat racing.

Jacobs served in the Luftwaffe in World War 2, but was noted for his anti-Nazi views – so much so that he had to live in Holland for a while, especially when he refused Hermann Göring the major shareholding in his aircraft company. By the time he died in Munich in July 1978, Jacobs was the last survivor of the 78 aviation recipients of the *Pour le Mérite*.

JASTA 12

This unit initally operated a few Fokker triplanes alongside Albatros D Vs in the early spring of 1918, but eventually became fully equipped with the Dr I. The most well known of these was 404/17, flown by its former *Staffelführer* Adolf Ritter von Tutschek, who by then was leader of JG II, which had *Jasta* 12 as part of its establishment.

Jagdgeschwader II was officially formed on 2 February 1918, with *Jagdstaffel* 12 based at Toulis. The *Jasta* marking of black tails was continued on the unit's triplanes, along with white engine cowlings – the latter marking later became common to all of JG II's Dr Is.

Von Tutschek, who was from Ingolstadt, in Bavaria, had achieved 23 victories by the summer of 1917, but a serious wound on 11 August ended his run. He returned to duty in February 1918 as commander of the newly-formed JG II. He first flew the Fokker triplane on the 17th of that month, and the next day he wrote in his diary, 'I pass the time with a Fokker triplane with a rotary engine. It climbs terrifically and is unbelievably mobile. In short, I find this machine most fantastic'.

On the 19th he flew his first patrol, in Dr I 216/17. His diary entries for 22 and 26 February are as follows;

'The new Fokker triplane I am flying is a tremendous machine . . . has marvellous manoeuvrability.

'(26 February) Today my first victim since my return to the front. At noon I am sitting in my Fokker, rocking from left wing to the right as I fly in the direction of Laon. I look down and see two black flak bursts, intended to alert me to something.

'Far in the distance there is an aircraft flying at an altitude of 2000 metres, heading inland, but at this distance I can't recognise the type. I cut him off, as I am higher and can therefore catch up rapidly. I can't see the markings, but I am suspicious, and with a jerk I pull my

A convivial grouping of JG II leader Adolf von Tutschek and his men (and mascots) of his old unit, *Jasta* 12, at their château at Toulis in February 1918. They are, from left to right, Ltn Oskar Müller (OzbV), Oblt Blumenbach (commander *Jasta* 12, 2 victories), Ltn Herbert Bock (rear), Ltn Hermann Becker (23, front), Vfw Ulrich Neckel (30, rear), Ltn Koch, Hptm von Tutschek (27), Ltn Hans Staats (1 victory), Oblt a D Krapfenbauer and Ltn Paul Hoffmann (1 victory) (*via VanWyngarden*)

triplane up vertically. I'm now above him, and can clearly see the English cockades.

'Bank around – left eye closed – cock the guns with the right hand. The Tommy, too, is laying into the curve, but with his heavy 200-hp SPAD he doesn't get around as fast. Without his being able to return the fire, my machine guns rattle.

'Fifty shots and the SPAD rears up vertically, but I am after him. Then down in a dive. I blink warily at my speedometer, which shows far above 240 km per hour. I stay close behind him. Never let loose before the crash is a principle I had adopted after learning the hard way.

'Now his propeller stops turning and a long white smoke trail points to a damaged gas tank. Now the SPAD lands, and to my great happiness stands there in good shape near Athies. I circle my prey until I see two riders come galloping up and take my opponent prisoner.'

The British PoW was 2Lt D C Doyle, who was happy to have escaped lightly with a grazing shot to the little toe – his SPAD XIII became a liberally photographed trophy of von Tutschek's 24th victory.

On 6 March von Tutschek led three triplanes and four Albatros fighters of *Jasta* 12 on a patrol, attacking a flight of seven SEs from No 24 Sqn over the Groupy woods. The *Geschwader* commander repeated the feat of forcing down an aircraft intact – this time the SE 5a of Lt A P Wigan.

Von Tutschek was again in action against No 24 Sqn on 15 March, but this time his luck failed him. He fell victim to a surprise attack from above. From various accounts it seems he was struck a glancing blow to the temple which may have rendered him unconscious – the triplane was seen to spiral down rapidly, and his pilots thought they saw it make a good landing. However, von Tutschek was later found dead in his machine.

Lt H B Redler, the South African pilot that fired at the Dr I, only claimed a probable, his fourth of an eventual ten victories.

Vzfw Ulrich Neckel and Leutnant der Reserve Hermann Becker were both *Jasta* 12 aces who are known to have flown the triplane in action. Twenty-year-old Neckel became an ace in early 1918, and probably scored a few triplane victories in March and early April 1918 before the D VII arrived. He ended the war with 30 victories, but only ten of these were scored whilst serving with *Jasta* 12. Having cheated death many times in combat, Neckel did not survive the tuberculosis that he

Von Tutschek's 404/17 is seen at Toulis on 15 March 1918. It has a black fuselage and tailplane aft of the national insignia and a white cowling. Earlier photographs of this machine show that it carried black and white streamers from the wing skids, and in this shot the starboard one can be seen wrapped around the interplane strut. Von Tutschek is standing in his RFC flying coat some yards in front of his machine. Behind von Tutschek and the clutch of mechanics is the No 23 Sqn SPAD XIII that he had brought down on 26 February for his 24th victory. Before this morning was over, von Tutschek would die whilst flying this machine in combat (*via VanWyngarden*)

Toulis again on 15 March 1918. The unit is in transition from the Albatros to the Dr I, and some pilots have two aircraft parked side-by-side. For example, the first two machines belong to Vzfw Ulrich Neckel, and bear his white chevron marking with a narrow black border. The sixth aircraft is the Dr I believed to have been used by Hermann Becker, whose score stood at six when this photograph was taken, and would eventually reach 23 (*via VanWyngarden*)

Ltn Hermann Becker, who flew with *Jasta* 12, survived the war with 23 victories (*via VanWyngarden*)

contracted post-war, and he died in 1928. He had received the 'Blue Max' in November 1918.

At 30 years of age in early 1918, Hermann Becker was one of the oldest pilots in the *Geschwader*. Having claimed a number of victories prior to the arrival of the Dr I, he effectively doubled his score with the triplane. Remaining with *Jasta* 12, Becker had claimed 23 kills in all by the end of the war. Although nominated for the *Pour le Mérite*, the ace's chances of receiving the award were dashed by the Armistice.

JASTA 13

A component of *Jagdgeschwader* II, this *Staffel* had received examples of the triplane by March 1918. Its Dr Is carried the unit marking of white engine cowlings and tails, with personal emblems marked on the fuselage between the cockpit and the white tail section.

Ltn Hans Martin Pippart certainly scored several of his 22 victories flying the Dr I in *Jasta* 13 in the spring of 1918. This 29-year-old had learnt to fly pre-war, and he even had his own small aircraft manufacturing company that he co-owned with Heinrich Noll in 1913, so it was natural for him to become a military pilot when war came.

Pippart was eventually assigned to *Fl Abt (A)* 220 on the Eastern Front in February 1916. In April 1917 provisional fighter detachment *Kampfstaffel* 1 was formed from this unit, and Pippart was assigned to it, flying a Roland D II. His first victory came on 25 May, and five more followed in the next six months – four out of his six victories were balloons.

Next, he joined *Jasta* 13 on the Western Front in December 1917 and continued adding to his score.

In the same 6 March fight with No 24 Sqn in which von Tutschek scored his final victory, Pippart downed another of the SEs for his 8th kill, and first in a triplane. On 30 March he attacked a Bréguet, but was forced to land when the French observer shot up the engine of his Dr I. Two days later, however, he succeeded in flaming a French balloon for his ninth victory, and last in *Jasta* 13 before transferring to *Jasta* 19, where he continued to fly the triplane.

JASTA 14

This *Staffel* flew triplanes under the leadership of Johannes (Hans) Werner, the unit receiving its first few examples of the type in January 1918 at Boncourt aerodrome, in the 7th Army sector.

It seems this *Jasta* was originally planned to be part of the establishment of JG II, hence its allocation of triplanes. Even though these plans later changed, Werner was allowed to retain the Dr Is, and *Jasta* 14 ended up operating triplanes longer than any other unit. Despite this longevity *Jasta* 14 was never fully equipped with the type, for there were always some Albatros D Vas, and later Fokker D VIIs, on strength as well.

The unit marking employed on the triplanes was a horizontal black/white stripe running the length of the fuselage. Besides Werner, the remaining *Jasta* 14 aces who undoubtedly flew the Dr I were Vzfw Paul Rothe and Leutnant der Reserve Herbert Boy, each with five victories. Ltn Hasso von Wedel flew Dr I 183/17, marked with his usual family crest marking, in this *Jasta*, but he failed to achieve any combat successes with the unit. He later commanded both *Jagdstaffeln* 75 and 24, and survived the war with five victories.

Ltn Werner flew both the Albatros D Va and the Dr I as *Staffelführer*, and one of his triplane victims was Australian ace Maj R S Dallas DSO, DSC. Although a ex-naval pilot, Dallas had been made CO of the RAF's No 40 Sqn in June 1918 following the merging of the RNAS and RFC.

During certain periods, squadron COs were not officially allowed to cross the lines for fear of losing valued and experienced commanders. On 1 June, however, Dallas was flying alone near the front, but staying clear of the actual trench system. He must have been spotted by Werner and two companions from the German side, and using cloud cover, they surprised the Australian, and shot him down. Dallas had scored over 30 kills.

He was Werner's sixth victim, to which he added one more in a Fokker D VII. His second Dr I – 583/17 – was brought down inside Allied lines on 9 June whilst being flown by a junior pilot from the *Jasta*, who was in turn captured.

In *Jasta* 14 personal emblems were usually painted aft of the cockpit, interrupting the black/white unit stripe marking. Occasionally, the cross insignia was also painted over, as was the case with 183/17, flown by Hasso von Wedel. A highly experienced two-seater pilot who was posted in during February 1918, his personal badge consisted of a red 'richtrad' – a medieval device for torture/execution! The fuselage cross was obscured with heavy olive-brown streaking which was indistinguishable from the factory camouflage. By war's end von Wedel had commanded *Jasta* 75, then *Jasta* 24 and finally *Jagdgruppe* 12. He survived the conflict with five confirmed victories (*A Imrie, HAC/UTD via Van Wyngarden*)

JASTA 15

Outside of Gontermann, whose exploits were detailed earlier, two other aces were known to have flown the Dr I with *Jasta* 15 – Leutnant der Reserve Kurt Monnington and Ltn Hans Müller.

A former infantryman, the 21-year-old Müller had scored three victories prior to the mass exchange of pilots with *Jasta* 18 in late March 1918. The German ace, and leader, Rudolf Berthold had been given command of JG II after von Tutschek's death, and such was his influence that he was able to exchange *Jasta* 15's personnel with *Jasta* 18 so that he could have his old unit as part of his new command!

Müller and Monnington briefly flew Dr Is from the *Jasta* 15 field at Autremencourt in early March, but did not have time to attain any victories on the type. The unit was forced to relinquish its few Dr Is when the great 'switch' took place, so most of the kills claimed by Monnington and Müller were achieved with the Fokker D VII in the following summer.

JASTA 19

A number of *Jasta* 19's aces are known to have flown triplanes, the unit having a full complement on strength in April as part of *Jagdgeschwader* II. Indeed, its Dr Is were the most colourful in the *Geschwader*, bearing the *Staffel* marking of diagonal yellow and black stripes on their tails, complemented by white cowlings. At first individual markings generally consisted of large yellow numerals on the fuselage, but *Staffelführer* Walter Göttsch instituted the use of white symbolic markings instead – the unit's triplanes universally had their fuselage cross insignia overpainted to facilitate the use of such emblems.

The Albatros D Va and Fokker Dr I of *Jasta* 14's leader, Ltn Johannes 'Hans' Werner. This photograph was taken in January 1918 to record the transfer of markings to his new triplane, 198/17. The unit's horizontal stripe was intersected by Werner's two personal stripes, all of which were apparently applied in the same colour. Werner achieved five of his seven victories in 1918, many of them no doubt in the Dr I – including the CO of No 40 Sqn, Australian ace Maj R S Dallas DSO DSC, on 1 June (*A Imrie, HAC/UTD, via Van Wyngarden*)

Leutnant der Reserve Walter Göttsch was a veteran air fighter come early 1918, having scored 17 victories by the time he arrived at the *Staffel*. Born in Altour, near Hamburg, in 1897, he had amassed a wealth of experience since first seeing active duty in 1915. He had compiled his victory tally while serving with *Jasta* 8, but in February 1918 Göttsch had been given command of *Jasta* 19. Here, he flew Fokker Dr I 202/17 and then 419/17, increasing his score to 20.

However, on 10 April (the day he claimed his last kill) he was hit by the return fire from the gunner of an RE 8 and he crashed to his death southeast of the Bois de Gentelles – German accounts state that Göttsch was hit by British ground fire. His fighter fell behind Allied lines, and the triplane – 419/17 – was given the British 'captured aircraft' number G 163. The RE 8 crew force-landed, but survived.

As noted earlier in this chapter, Göttsch was succeeded as commander by Hans Pippart, who had transferred in from *Jasta* 13, and who had flown 471/17 with *Jasta* 19. Two days after taking command he downed a Bréguet for his tenth confirmed claim, on 20 April. He added four more to his tally in May, and perhaps another on 12 June in the triplane, prior to the arrival of the Fokker biplanes.

Dr Is from *Jasta* 19 line-up at Balâtre airfield. Arthur Rahn's 433/17 can be seen at far right, while Rudolf Rienau's 503/17 is third from the right (*via VanWyngarden*)

Pippart was awarded the prestigious 'Hohenzollern' on 2 May, and brought his final score to 22 on 11 August, but was killed in action later that same day.

Dr I 433/17 of *Jasta* 19's Arthur Rahn is one of the war's most familiar triplanes due to its prominent location in a classic official *Kogenluft* photograph. Leutnant der Reserve Rahn learned some of his skills as a *Jagdflieger* under the stern leadership of Rudolf Berthold in

Ltn Walter Göttsch sits on the cockpit sill of his second Dr I, 419/17 – this machine was identified by a white swastika on the fuselage. Eventually, the interplane struts and the upper surface of the top wing would be painted in the pilot's personal white colour to enhance identification of the commander's machine. Göttsch died in this machine on 10 April 1918 following an attack on an RE 8 of No 52 Sqn. The ace was fatally hit either by a round from the observer's Lewis gun, or by fire from the British trenches (*via VanWyngarden*)

As a component of JG II, *Jasta* 19 received its first consignment of Fokker triplanes in February 1918. One was 202/17, flown by the leader, Ltn Walter Göttsch. Initially some of the unit's triplanes bore large yellow individual numbers aft of the cockpit, 202/17 being marked accordingly with the number '2', which was repeated on the top decking. Since this obscured the original serial number legend, this was reapplied in yellow block letters beneath the tailplane. The *Geschwader* marking of a white engine cowling was augmented by angled yellow and black bands on both surfaces of the tailplane (*via VanWyngarden*)

Following the death of Walter Göttsch, command of *Jasta* 19 was passed to Hans Pippart from *Jasta* 13. He is seen here with his *Jasta* 19 Dr I 471/17, which apparently had all of its upper surfaces (wings included) painted in a dark solid colour (black?). The cowling remained white and the unit's yellow/black tail colours were no doubt retained. Not visible in this view is Pippart's personal emblem of a light-coloured (yellow?) disc, which was eventually marked on both fuselage sides and the upper decking, as well as on the centre section of the top wing (*HAC/UTD via VanWyngarden*)

Jasta 19's Ltn Arthur Rahn is seen seated in the cockpit of his 433/17, which has been decorated with his personal emblem of a band of white diamonds bordered by two white bands. This decoration was applied directly against the streaky olive-brown camouflage. Rahn had also used this marking on the Albatros D V that he had previously flown with *Jasta* 18. Note the small windscreen and rear-view mirror. Rahn survived the war with six victories, the last two of which were probably achieved in the Dr I (*HAC/UTD via VanWyngarden*)

Staffeln 18 and 15, before transferring to *Jasta* 19 on 29 April. He may well have scored two or three of his six victories with 433/17 in April and May 1918 – he survived the war.

Leutnant der Reserve Rudolf Rienau may have also opened his account with a triplane, as his first victory was claimed on 6 March 1918. The former infantryman had briefly served in *Jasta* 1 prior to joining 19 in October 1917. He flew Dr I 504/17, and scored six victories during the war, although only his first one or two were probably achieved with the triplane. Rienau became a flight instructor after the war and died in an accident in 1925.

Hans Körner had achieved three victories in 1917, serving in *Jasta* 8 alongside Walter Göttsch. When the latter took command of *Jasta* 19 in February 1918, he requested Körner's transfer to his new unit. Körner

Fokker Dr I 504/17 was the mount of *Jasta* 19's 19-year-old six-victory ace Ltn Rudolf Rienau, who would eventually command the unit. He scored at least his first victory flying the triplane. The white candy stripes on the fuselage certainly served as personal identification, but they may also have been another attempt to misdirect the aim of an opponent glued to the aircraft's tail during a dogfight
(*via VanWyngarden*)

flew 503/17, but probably only added one kill to his tally in the triplane – his score eventually reached seven. He was killed after the war in a motorcycle crash.

JASTA 26

A component of *Jagdgeschwader* III, this *Staffel* was fully equipped with the Dr I by early April 1918, and several of its aces saw combat with the triplane.

Vzfw Otto Esswein's machine was 426/17, but by the time he received it his score had already reached eight. Rewarded for this success, the 28-year-old Württemberger received the Württemberg Gold and Silver Military Merit Badges, as well as the Golden Military Merit Cross (considered the *Pour le Mérite* for NCOs) on 3 June 1918. Esswein probably scored two kills with a triplane in March, and perhaps also his final two on the last day of May, which brought his score to 12. By mid-June the Dr Is were gone from the *Jasta*.

Rudolf Rienau precariously seated on the cockpit sill of his candy-striped triplane
(*via Franks collection*)

Blemished but nevertheless interesting view of *Jasta* 19's Ltn Hans Körner and his Dr I (503/17), emblazoned with a white zig-zag lightning bolt emblem which ended in an arrow-head point beneath the tailplane. Note the Oigee telescopic sight fitted between the two machine guns. Rienau's striped triplane can also be seen at the extreme left of the photograph. Körner transferred in from *Jasta* 8 at the request of Ltn Göttsch, and probably scored one of his eventual seven kills in the Dr I (*A Imrie HAC/UTD/via VanWyngarden*)

These Dr Is from *Jasta* 26 were photographed lined up at Erchin airfield in early April 1918. Only two appear to be bedecked with the *Staffel's* black and white bands on the fuselage and tailplane. A few have also had their crosses changed to *Balkenkreuz*. The aircraft at the extreme left was flown by *Staffelführer* Ltn Fritz Loerzer, and is fully marked in unit colours, including a black cowling. This machine also bore a cast aluminium plate (with the pilot's initials 'FL') attached to the face plate of the cowling. Finally, note its black wheel covers (*via VanWyngarden*)

Three vizfeldwebel aces of *Jasta* 26 pose with the unit's new triplanes in early April 1918. To the left is Fritz Classen, who probably scored two of his eleven kills in the Dr I. In the middle is the formidable Otto Fruhner, who, after being commissioned and credited with 27 victories, missed being awarded the 'Blue Max' due to the Kaiser's abdication! And to the right, in front of his own triplane (426/17), is Otto Esswein. The last two of his twelve victories were scored in the Dr I on 31 May. The white panel aft of the cockpit on 426/17 would soon be decorated with Esswein's 'E' initial, which was repeated on the top wing centre section. The position of the flare cartridge rack and signal pistol on the left side of the cockpit was fairly standard in this unit (*via VanWyngarden*)

Esswein did not score again, and was killed in action on 21 July. He had survived a bail-out just five days earlier.

Jagdstaffel 26 leader Ltn Fritz Loerzer, whose more famous brother Bruno was the commander of JG II, also flew triplanes. However, Fritz had only scored once or twice in his Dr I when he was taken prisoner on 12 June 1918 – his tally then stood at 11 victories. Other aces that flew the Dr I with *Jasta* 26 were Erich Buder (12 victories), Fritz Classen (11) and Helmut Lange (9). All scored the odd kill with the triplane, and one noted victory was scored on 8 May 1918, when the *Jasta* surprised five SE 5a fighters of No 74 Sqn, whose pilots were strafing troops on the ground. The *Staffelführer* Loerzer, Buder, Classen and Lange each claimed a kill apiece, although the RAF squadron lost only three SE 5as, and had two others severely shot up.

Jasta 26's unit marking consisted of broad black and white bands encircling the fuselage and tail, with a black engine cowling.

JASTA 27

This unit was led by Oblt Hermann Göring between May 1917 and July 1918, during which time he received the *Pour le Mérite* following his 18th victory in April 1918. Again the *Staffel* used a variety of aircraft types, but Göring did fly the Dr I on several occasions, one mount being 206/17.

His personal war records were quite detailed up until late 1917, then became sparse. This is a pity, as it is impossible to be sure when he flew his triplane in combat. However, there are enough photographs of his

Dubbed the 'Flying Pastor', *Jasta* 26's Ltn Fritz Loerzer stands in front of his Dr I. This aircraft displays the unit colours of black/white bands from nose to tail, although the white panel adjacent to the cockpit is already begrimed and worn. Loerzer's triplane reportedly had the leading third of its upper wing surface painted black as a marking to identify him. Indeed, the black-coloured leading edge of the top wing is evident in this photograph – the entire centre section was also painted a similar colour. The younger brother of JG III's *Kommandeur*, Bruno Loerzer, Fritz achieved 11 victories. On 8 May he led his *Staffel* down to intercept a patrol of five SE 5a fighters from No 74 Sqn, three of which were subsequently destroyed (one by Loerzer) and two badly shot up. Loerzer was in turn shot down and taken prisoner on 12 June by the Australian Flying Corps' No 2 Sqn (*HAC/UTD via VanWyngarden*)

Dreidecker to be certain that he used it fairly frequently in the spring of 1918, even as the new Fokker D VIIs were starting to arrive.

Although we have a very coloured view of Göring because of his later life, there is no doubt that he was no slouch in World War 1 as regards combat. After initially seeing action with the army, he flew with the air service throughout the war in everything from two-seaters to the Fokker D VII, and finally commanding Richthofen's old JG I.

Göring's 22 claims bear testimony to his prowess as a fighter ace, although a few of these are suspect. However, he is not unique in this, and there is ample evidence that he was an effective *Jasta* and *Geschwader* leader in the Great War.

Another Fokker triplane used by *Jasta* 27 was 577/17, flown by Rudolf Klimke. This 27-year-old came from Merseberg, and had begun his war with the artillery, which he had joined in 1910. Joining the air service in 1915 he went through two-seaters – even bombing London at night in May 1916 – on to fighters, and by mid-1917 was with *Jasta* 27.

His score had risen to six by the time the Fokker triplane became available and he had the opportunity of adding two or three scalps to his tally before the Fokker D VII arrived. Klimke was wounded in September 1918, which ended his war, with a score of 17.

One of Klimke's fellow *Jasta* 27 aces was Ltn Helmuth Dilthey, who claimed six victories with the *Staffel*, but attained all of them at the controls of an Albatros D III or D V. Concerning his unit's equipment, he wrote in 1918;

Hermann Göring glares at the camera from the cockpit of one of his *Jasta* 27 triplanes – possibly 206/17. The struts are clearly decorated in his personal white colour, which was also applied to the tail, while other triplanes in his unit carried yellow cowlings and struts. A sheet metal baffle to deflect spent cartridge cases can be seen just aft of the ammunition belt guide (*via VanWyngarden*)

'It became somewhat better when we received the triplanes. At this time these were really no longer as good as the English single- and two-seaters – above all they were too slow and their motors too sensitive. But other than that, they were quite lovely. Our triplanes had yellow cowlings, yellow wing struts and yellow tails, and the rest was in a natural (factory-finish) colour. Only Oblt Göring's leader's aircraft had a white tail and a white cowling.'

This view of the *Jasta* 27 ace Rudolf Klimke provides a fairly clear look at his anchor insignia on the yellow tailplane of 577/17 – the anchor was a good luck talisman suggested by his mother. The black-coloured leading edge of the top wing is evident. Klimke scored the bulk of 16 victories either with Albatros fighters or the Fokker D VII (*HAC/UTD via VanWyngarden*)

JASTA 34B

Another ace photographed with a triplane is Rudolf Stark, although it is again unlikely that he scored any victories in one. There is little doubt that the triplane initially found great favour with the Bavarian pilots of *Jasta* 34, saddled as they were with second-rate Pfalz and Albatros machines.

Stark himself wrote in his book *Wings of War* about the arrival of the triplane in May 1918, by which time he had five official victories;

'At last we too are going to get better machines – Fokker triplanes. It is true that they are discarded machines of the *Jagdgeschwader* (I), and therefore contain quite a lot of hidden snags, but that does not diminish our joy. Three of them have already turned up. There is great competition as to who is to fly them, and finally we let the dice decide.

'At first we find these new machines a bit strange to fly, but they are extremely sensitive to the controls and rise up in the air like a lift. You can climb a few hundred metres in the twinkling of a second, and can then go round and round one spot like a top.'

However, before this 21-year-old Bavarian could score any victories in the triplane he was moved to command *Jasta* 77, and later still *Jasta* 35b. He ended the war with a possible 11 victories, with a number of others unconfirmed.

Robert Greim, was a 24-year-old Bavarian from Bayreuth, the son of a police captain. An army cadet pre-war, he was with the artillery in the

An unidentified Fokker Dr I and Albatros D V are presumably seen with their pilot and groundcrew. Both machines have fuselage bands, but in differing styles and colours. These aircraft look very much like *Jasta* 27 machines, as both seem to be painted in what could be the unit's markings. Additionally, this *Jasta* was one of the few to have photographs taken during its transition from the Albatros to Dr I (*via Franks collection*)

Jasta 34b's Ltn Rudolf Stark, seated in his Dr I 146/17. An ex-*Jasta* 11 machine, it still wore red markings when issued to Stark, and it is doubtful if his individual emblem (a lilac band) was ever applied to the triplane. Indeed, this machine was later flown by Oblt Greim, and then by Ltn August Delling (*A Imrie/HAC /UTD via VanWyngarden*)

Rudolf Stark again, this time standing alongside triplane 146/17 on 14 May 1918. The aircraft had only just arrived from JG I when this photograph was taken (*A Imrie/ HAC/UTD/via VanWyngarden*)

early part of the war, transferring to the *Fliegertruppe* in August 1915. Flying two-seaters, then fighters with *Jasta* 34b, his score had risen to a dozen by the spring of 1918, at which time he was in command of *Jagdgruppe* 10, as well as *Jasta* 34b.

Greim flew triplane 521/17 for a while, and on 27 June 1918, during a fight with a Bristol Fighter, his machine lost its cowling, which struck and damaged his top wing and lower port interplane strut as it flew off, but he got it down safely.

He later commanded *Jagdgruppe* 9, ending the war with 28 victories. Awarded the *Pour le Mérite* in early October, and the Bavarian *Max-Joseph Order* later in that month, making him a Knight (Ritter), he thus added the title 'von' to his name. He committed suicide on 24 May 1945 as a General Feldmarschall, and acting commander of the Luftwaffe, following Germany's defeat.

Johan Pütz also saw service with *Jasta* 34b, gaining seven victories with the unit. Like other triplanes used by the *Jasta*, his was a former JG I aircraft which had been discarded with the arrival of the Fokker D VII. Pütz flew his during May and June, and may have scored one victory in it. He was posted away from the front in September 1918.

At least some of the unit's triplanes displayed the *Staffel's* silver-white rear fuselage and tailplane.

JASTA 36

This JG III unit would ultimately fly the triplane longer than most *Jastas* within the *Geschwader*. Along with *Jasta* Boelcke, the *Staffel* received its first triplanes at the end of January 1918, and still had some of its blue-nosed Dr Is on strength as late as August.

Due to the type's longevity of service, most of the unit's aces probably had some time on the Dr I during the final year of the war. One such individual was 26-year-old Heinrich Bongartz from Gelsenkirchen, Westphalia, was a

Bavarian *Jasta* 34 obtained its first triplanes in May 1918 at Foucaucourt. These were all ex-JG I machines that had been given up upon the arrival of D VII biplanes. *Jasta* 34b commander, Oblt Robert Greim (later Ritter von Greim), is seen here with his Dr I 521/17 in June. This aircraft bore the full *Staffel* marking of a whitish-silver fuselage from the cockpit aft to the tail, including the tailplane and elevators. This finish was applied to most of the unit's triplanes. The rudder remained white, and Greim's traditional personal marking of two red bands is also clearly evident. This red colour was also applied to the cowling, and perhaps to the wheel covers as well. *Jasta* 34b's pilots had looked forward to the arrival of the triplane, but engine trouble with these second-hand machines quickly dampened their enthusiasm, and as soon as the D VII arrived the remaining Dr Is soon went out of favour (*via VanWyngarden*)

Jasta 34b's seven-victory ace Vfw Johann Pütz stands in front of his personally-marked Dr I. His individual decoration consisted of two green bands aft of the cockpit, with the fighter's engine cowling in the same colour. Otherwise, this aircraft boasts a scheme very similarly to Greim's Dr I. Pütz is seen wearing a prized RFC Sidcot flying suit (*HAC/UTD via VanWyngarden*)

former school teacher and infantryman who began flying with *Jasta* 36 in 1917 – he first scored during 'Bloody April'. His tally stood at over 30 by the time the triplane became available, and he had been *Staffelführer* since September. His *Pour le Mérite* had been awarded just before Christmas.

Flying 441/17 on 30 March 1918, Bongartz was hit by AA fire. Although he got down safely, he nosed over, damaging the engine, cowling and leading edge of the top wing. He had a reserve machine, however (575/17), and he was flying this on 29 April when he got into a dogfight with several RAF aircraft. Hit in the head by a bullet which passed through his left temple, eye and nose, Bongartz crash-landed virtually unconscious near Kemmel Hill, his Dr I riddled with bullet holes – there were nearly 40 in the engine cowling alone. This obviously put him out of the war.

Bongartz' final score was 33, the last three of which were probably achieved in his triplane. He had been shot down by No 74 Sqn's Capt C G Glynn, flying an SE 5a. An infantry eyewitness to Bongartz' crash was later quoted in Walter Zuerl's book *Pour le Mérite Flieger*;

'This afternoon a Fokker triplane came down, overturned, and the pilot came crawling out from under it with one eye shot away, blood streaming out of it. First he walked around and took a look at his machine, then came over to us with his eye hanging down and introduced himself: "Leutnant Bongartz", with a bow.

'We bandaged him up and I immediately called for a car – he was in terrible pain, as the bullet had penetrated his temple and lodged in his nose, and he couldn't breathe through his nose. He just said, "Ja, Ja, we all take our turn".

'A famous English naval squadron (sic) had surprised him in the clouds. His aircraft was shot to pieces and spattered with blood. He was still able to land and walk, even with his terrible wound, but not for long.

He was given a shot of morphine and then he rested quietly. He was lucky that's for sure, even though he couldn't fly any more.'

Bongartz died of a heart attack in 1946, just prior to his 54th birthday.

THE END

Despite the popular impression that the Fokker triplane filled the war-torn skies of France in World War 1, its period in the frontline was brief, and the number in combat was small. And although Manfred von Richthofen had used it to advantage, he was well aware of its short-comings – confidence in the machine was not advanced by its structural problems. The Dr I simply did not live up to expectations.

By the hot summer days of June 1918, the triplane's rotary engine was suffering from overheating due to the poor-quality *ersatz* castor oil then in use, and engine failure was a common complaint. By then, too, Allied pilots had learnt how to deal with the Dr I, utilising mass diving attacks from altitude. As long as they refused to dogfight the triplane on its own terms, the superior ceiling and speed of the Allied machines led to the demise of the Dr I as an effective fighter.

Even before the big March Offensive, von Richthofen knew of the coming of the Fokker D VII, and knew too that oil for rotary engines was now far from satisfactory – so much so that he voiced his opinion to 'higher authority' that he felt the day of the rotary engine was fast coming to an end. He wanted the Fokker D VII biplane, with its water-cooled engine – either BMW or Mercedes. The D VIIs were on their way, but would not reach the Front until after the Baron's death in battle.

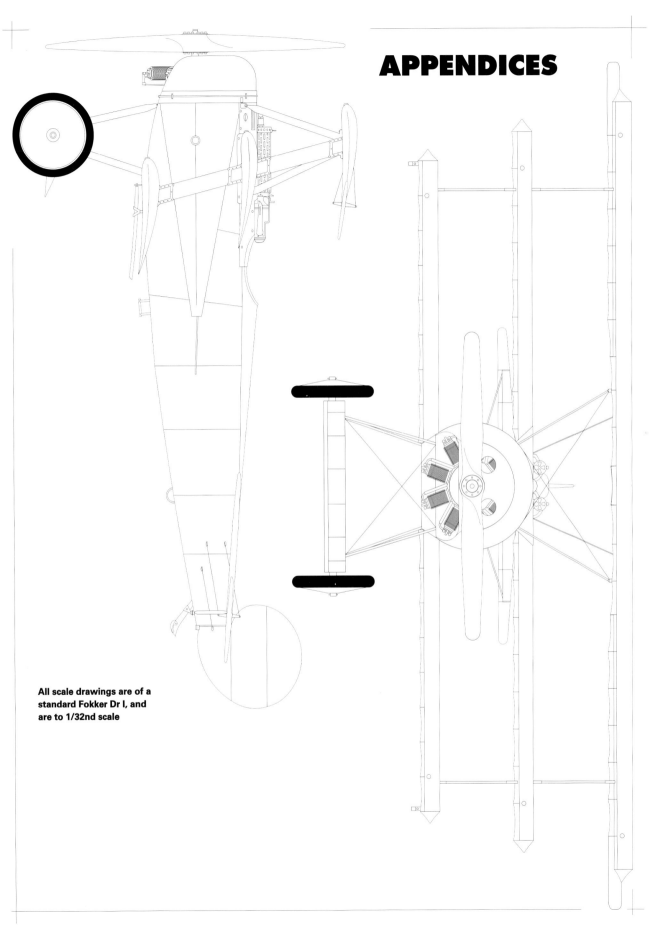

APPENDICES

All scale drawings are of a
standard Fokker Dr I, and
are to 1/32nd scale

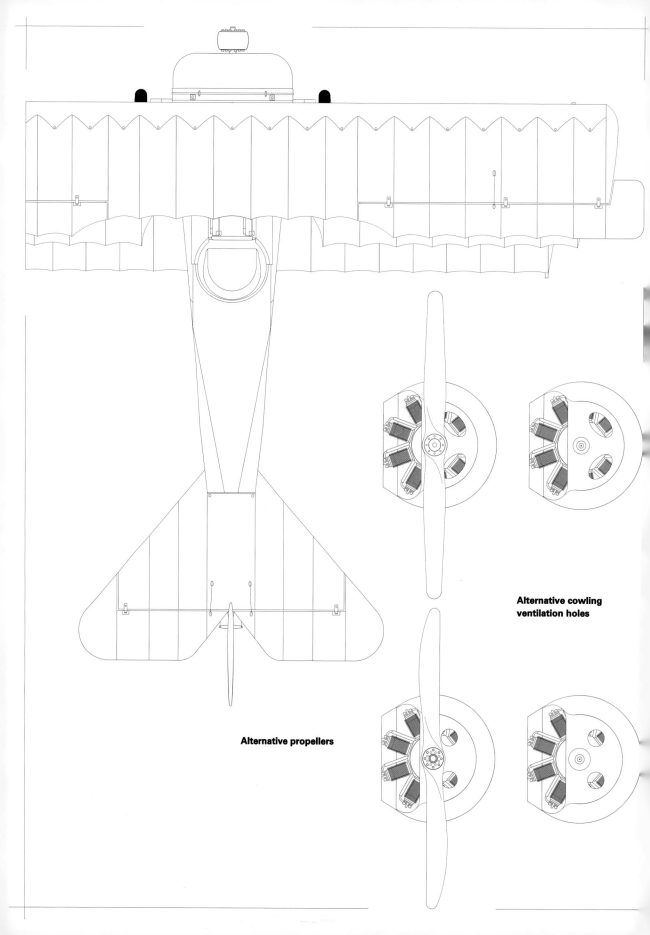

Alternative propellers

**Alternative cowling
ventilation holes**

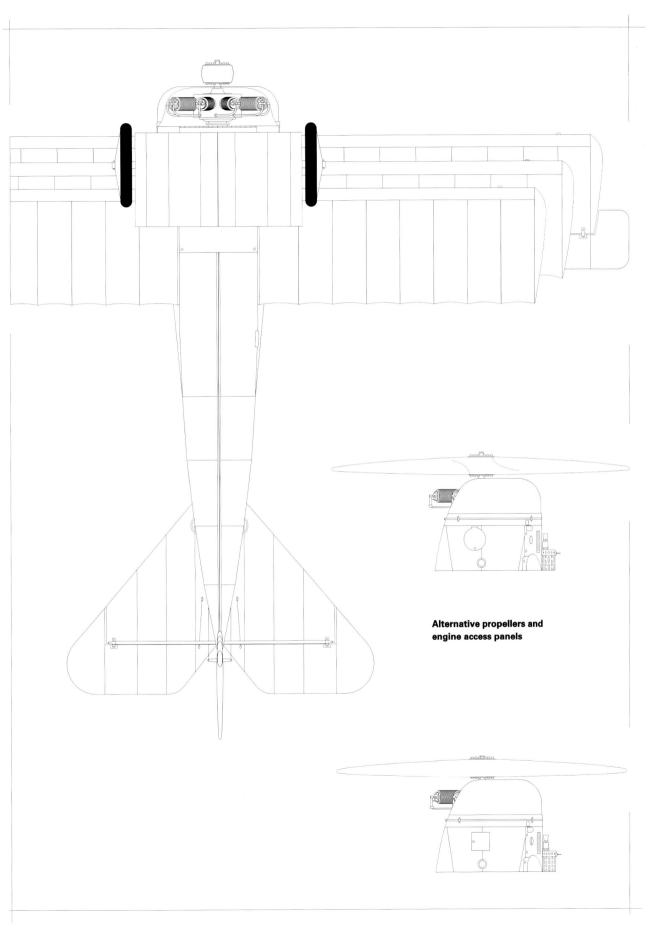

**Alternative propellers and
engine access panels**

COLOUR PLATES

All the artwork in this colour section has been specially commissioned for this volume, and artist Harry Dempsey has worked with the authors to illustrate the aircraft as accurately as possible, given the limited information available after the passage of 80 years. The research of Paul Leaman, Alex Imrie and Ray Rimell was of great value in compiling this work.

1

Fokker F I 102/17 of Rittm Manfred von Richthofen and Oblt Kurt Wolff, *Jasta* 11, Marckebeeke, September 1917

F I 102/17 was presented to von Richthofen of JG I in August 1917, and Oblt Kurt Wolff was shot down in this aircraft and killed on 15 September. Pre-production F Is were given a factory finish of overall light blue-grey, streaked in olive-brown dope on all uppersurfaces, to effect a camouflage, with undersides and struts light blue. Engine cowling and wheel covers were probably solid olive-brown. The factory-applied works number 1729 was marked at the bottom of the rudder.

2

Fokker F I 103/17 of Ltn Werner Voss, *Jasta* 10, Marcke, September 1917

F I 103/17 (Wk-Nr 1730 on rudder) was flown by Werner Voss, leader of *Jasta* 10. This F I bore a factory finish identical to that of 102/17. The cowling colour may have been factory-finish olive or *Jasta* 10 yellow, with either being equally likely. The rudder was definitely white.

3

Fokker Dr I 152/17 of Rittm Manfred von Richthofen, JG I, Avesnes-le-Sec, March 1918

Dr I 152/17 displayed a red cowling, upper wing, tail, struts and wheel covers, whilst the rest of the machine bore a factory finish of olive-brown streaking over clear-doped linen on uppersurfaces, and blue-grey undersurfaces. This is the colour scheme contemporary observers described for Richthofen's 'reserve' machines.

4

Fokker Dr I 454/17 of Ltn Lothar von Richthofen, *Jasta* 11, Avesnes-le-Sec, March 1918

Lothar's Dr I 454/17 (Wk-Nr 2079) was painted in his personal yellow colour. Red cowling, struts and wheel covers denoted the unit, while the upper wing, rear fuselage and tailplane were yellow. This overpainting was, in places, thinly applied, allowing some of the camouflage and solid-olive cross fields to show through as a darker yellow.

5

Fokker Dr I (serial unconfirmed) of Ltn Werner Steinhäuser, *Jasta* 11, Avesnes-le-Sec, February 1918

Steinhäuser's Dr I displayed the *Jasta* red in the usual locations – on the front of the cowling, 'eyes' were painted around the cooling holes, probably in yellow. Steinhäuser's former regimental colours were displayed as a yellow 'X' on a red fuselage band, and the rudder was white. Standard camouflage finish otherwise, and tailplane markings, if any, cannot be seen. This Dr I had early style ailerons.

6

Fokker Dr I 588/17 of Ltn Richard Wenzl, *Jasta* 11, Cappy, April 1918

Wenzl's Dr I bore the usual streaky green-brown camouflage and unit markings in red. His personal marking was a white and black fuselage band in the proportions of the Iron Cross ribbon, with colours reversed. Solid olive was applied to cover the white cross fields, and *Balkenkreuze* were applied. The leading edges of the wings were picked out in black/white. Serial number 588/17 was reportedly repainted just forward of the vertical arm of the fuselage cross, although the number 178 was seen on the port elevator.

7

Fokker Dr I 545/17 of Ltn Hans Weiss, *Jasta* 11, Cappy, April/May 1918

Much of Weiss's 545/17 (Wk-Nr 2213 on rudder) was, as his name implies, white. Other than the usual streaky camouflage, the whole of the tail and rear fuselage was white, which extended up the fuselage decking to the cockpit. The uppersurface of the top wing was white as well, with red unit markings in typical style.

8

Fokker Dr I 425/17 of Rittm Manfred von Richthofen, JG I, Léchelle, March 1918

JG I commander Richthofen's Dr I 425/17 (Wk-Nr 2009) was one of the few aircraft that the Rittmeister flew that was actually all-red – the smooth finish evident in photographs suggests it may have been painted this way at the factory. When photographed at Léchelle in late March 1918, it was marked with white-bordered iron cross insignia as illustrated.

9

Fokker Dr I 564/17 of Ltn Werner Steinhäuser, *Jasta* 11, Cappy, April 1918

This Dr I also bore Steinhäuser's red and yellow colours, this time as a red 'X' on a yellow band, with the usual *Staffel* red markings. The tailplane was also decorated with personal red stripes on a yellow field, which are provisionally illustrated. Two styles of *Balkenkreuze* were borne on the wings and fuselage. The rudder may still have displayed the Wk-Nr 2234.

10

Fokker Dr I 425/17 of Rittm Manfred von Richthofen, JG I, Cappy, April 1918

Following the introduction of the *Balkenkreuze* (sometimes called Latin crosses), the markings of 425/17 were amended twice. The colour plate depicts the Dr I in its final appearance, with narrow-chord cross bars and a white rudder. The surviving crosses from this machine appear quite crude, due mostly to ageing and the two earlier crosses showing through the various deteriorated coats of paint.

11

Fokker Dr I 204/17 of Vzfw Paul Bäumer of *Jasta* Boelcke, Marcke, early March 1918

Bäumer first flew Dr I 204/17 (Wk-Nr 1923) from Marcke in

early March. Besides the normal streaky camouflage, it carried the *Jasta* Boelcke marking of a black cowling with a white face plate, as well as black cabane struts with white tips and black wheel covers. The white rudder was edged in black, and a partially-completed thin black cross border was seen on the starboard side of the rudder at least. The *Staffel* markings also consisted of the tailplane and adjacent rear fuselage area painted half black and half white. This Dr I also bore the iron cross insignia on the upper surface of the bottom wings and in the centre of the tailplane. Bäumer's personal emblem was the red-white-black fuselage stripe.

12

Fokker Dr I 190/17 of Ltn Otto Löffler, *Jasta* Boelcke, Marcke, March 1918

Löffler's Dr I (Wk-Nr 1908) was painted with the usual *Jasta* Boelcke markings on its cowling and tail in the Prussian black and white colours. His personal emblem was a fuselage band in lemon yellow (the colour of his former grenadier regiment) edged in white. Standard finish otherwise – like many other Dr Is of this unit, auxiliary undercarriage struts were fitted.

13

Fokker Dr I 195/17 of Ltn Hermann Vallendor, *Jasta* Boelcke, Halluin-Ost, May 1918

Vallendor first flew this Dr I from Marcke in March 1918. It was marked and camouflaged in a similar vein to other *Jasta* Boelcke machines, with the addition of black wheel covers. His personal marking was a large 'V' on the fuselage sides and top, and also on the centre section of the upper wing.

14

Fokker Dr I 413/17 of Oblt Karl Bolle, *Jasta* Boelcke, Halluin-Ost, May 1918

This Dr I (Wk-Nr 1997) was the mount of *Jasta* CO, Oblt Bolle. It too carried the standard camouflage and black/white markings. The pilot's personal symbol was a yellow (again, the colour of his former regiment) band edged with black and white striping. The rudder also had a black edging, and the fighter was fitted with an Oigee telescopic sight.

15

Fokker Dr I (serial unconfirmed) of Ltn Hermann Frommherz, *Jasta* Boelcke, Halluin-Ost, circa May 1918

This Dr I was distinctive in its black and white diamond pattern fuselage band and interplane struts. The black/white *Staffel* tail marking was reversed from those seen previously, with starboard side in white and the port black. When photographed this Dr I did not have the usual white face plate on the black(?) cowling. The rudder had a black border.

16

Fokker Dr I 204/17 of Vzfw Paul Bäumer, *Jasta* Boelcke, Halluin-Ost, circa May 1918

By this time 204/17 had undergone a change in markings. Not only were *Balkenkreuze* applied in all locations, but the tips of all three wings were painted black, with a narrow white/red border. The red border on the uppersurface of the top wing was absent, and the crosses were apparently displayed on a white field. The tailplane cross was retained, but those insignia atop of the lower wing were painted over.

17

Fokker Dr I 586/17 of Ltn Ernst Udet, *Jasta* 4, Beugneux-Cramoiselle, June 1918

Formerly the mount of Ltn Kirschstein (see Plate 21), this Dr I was later taken over by Udet. It remained marked with Kirschstein's stripes, but was now personalised with Udet's *LO!* insignia on the fuselage, in honour of his fiancée.

18

Fokker Dr I 139/17 of Vzfw Josef Mai, *Jasta* 5, Cappy, May 1918

Dr I 139/17 (Wk-Nr 1850) was an ex-*Jasta* 11 machine transferred to *Jasta* 5 – cowling, cabane and undercarriage struts and wheel covers probably remained red, with olive interplane struts. Most of the aircraft's uppersurfaces was finished in standard camouflage, with a previous circle marking on the fuselage now over-painted olive. The horizontal fuselage band was retained, along with a 'new' vertical white band, the entire machine presenting a worn and stained look. The rear fuselage and tail were overpainted, possibly in *Jasta* 5 green.

19

Fokker Dr I 403/17 of Ltn Johann Janzen, *Jasta* 6, Lieu St Amand, circa March 1918

This Dr I bore *Jasta* 6's classic black and white stripes on its horizontal tail surfaces, along with a black cowling and Janzen's personal emblem of a white 'snakeline' on a black fuselage band, bordered in white on its leading edge. The Wk-Nr 1987 on the rudder was obscured when that component was painted black to produce the white cross border.

20

Fokker Dr I 595/17(?) of Vzfw Franz Hemer, *Jasta* 6, Cappy, circa May 1918

The serial number of Hemer's Dr I is not confirmed, but it bore the usual *Staffel* colours on its cowling and tail, along with a white (or *very* light yellow) wavy line on its fuselage. Known as *'Locken'* to his fellow pilots due to his blond wavy hair, Hemer's insignia stemmed from his nickname.

21

Fokker Dr I 586/17 of Ltn Hans Kirschstein, *Jasta* 6, Cappy, circa April 1918

This view depicts the starboard side of Kirschstein's 'optical illusion', so-named because the diagonally painted black/white stripes were thought to put attacking pilots off their aim. The fuselage stripes were not mirror images, and they terminated at a vertical line at the cockpit. The white paint used was of poor quality, quickly staining with oil and exhaust deposits.

22

Fokker Dr I 450/17 of Ltn Josef Jacobs, *Jasta* 7, Ste Marguerite, May 1918

Jacobs flew 450/17 from March through to October 1918. It was marked with his fire-breathing devil's head (the illustration is based on Jacobs' own sketches and a photo), and bore crosses on the upper side of the bottom wing.

23

Fokker Dr I (serial unconfirmed) of Ltn Josef Jacobs, Ste Marguerite, circa September 1918

In addition to 450/17, Jacobs also flew 470/17, but the combat report descriptions for the latter do not match this machine, which bore white crosses on the wings and fuselage, and a black cross on a white rudder. This may have been the *third* Triplane mentioned by Jacobs in his final years.

24

Fokker Dr I 404/17 of Hptm Adolf von Tutschek, JG II, Toulis, March 1918

As leader of JG II, von Tutschek continued to fly with his old unit *Jasta* 12, and his Dr I was marked accordingly. It is depicted in its final stage of decoration, with an all-black tail and white cowling. The white cross fields on the upper wing (and perhaps the lower) were also reduced with black to produce a 5-cm white border. Black and white streamers were attached to both lower wings.

25

Fokker Dr I (serial unconfirmed) of Ltn Hermann Becker, *Jasta* 12, Toulis, March 1918

This machine, marked with a personal emblem of a black/white quartering, is seen in the famous photos of the *Jasta* 12 line-up at Toulis on 15 March 1918. It bore the usual *Staffel* markings of a black tail and white cowling – at the time of the photos, it retained the full white cross backgrounds on the upper wing. In the 1960s, Becker told an interviewer that this was indeed his aircraft. It survived in the unit until June, by which time it had undergone several changes in insignia.

26

Fokker Dr I (serial unconfirmed) of Vzfw Ulrich Neckel, *Jasta* 12, Balatre, April 1918

Also seen at Toulis, this Dr I bore Neckel's emblem of a white chevron with a thin black border, along with the typical *Jasta* 12 colours. This machine would also survive for some time, its national markings being altered to early full-bordered *Balkenkreuz* format and its rudder painted white.

27

Fokker Dr I (serial unconfirmed) of Ltn Hans Pippart, *Jasta* 13, Reneuil-Ferme, March 1918

Though once again the serial is obscured, this machine's white tail and cowling help identify it as a *Jasta* 13 Dr I. The white wavy line was Pippart's personal emblem. The rest of the aircraft being apparently factory-finish streaked camouflage, with complete white cross fields on the upper wing.

28

Fokker Dr I 198/17 of Ltn Hans Werner, *Jasta* 14, Boncourt, January 1918

Staffelführer Werner's Dr I 198/17 (Wk-Nr 1916 on the rudder) displayed the unit marking of two black and white stripes lengthways along the fuselage. His personalisation of the aircraft was to bisect this with two vertical bands of the same colours. Werner later had another Dr I (583/17) marked identically, save for *Balkenkreuze* on the fuselage and rudder.

29

Fokker Dr I 202/17 of Ltn Walter Göttsch, *Jasta* 19, Cuirieux, circa February 1918

Some of the first Dr Is supplied to *Jasta* 19 were marked with large yellow numerals on the fuselage sides as personal emblems, and unit CO Göttsch flew '2' for a short period. The white cowling and yellow/black angled bands on the tailplane were the unit marking of this *Staffel*. Since the painting of the yellow '2' obscured the serial number, this was unusually re-applied on the aft fuselage beneath the tailplane in yellow block characters. The cabane struts were apparently solid olive, with Wk-Nr '1921' stencilled on them in white, while the interplane struts were the usual undersurface blue.

30

Fokker Dr I 419/17 of Ltn Walter Göttsch, *Jasta* 19, Balatre, April 1918

By April Göttsch had instituted the overpainting of the fuselage crosses in a streaked camouflage virtually identical to the factory finish, and the application of white personal emblems. His own Dr I (Wk-Nr 2003, which is again stencilled on the olive cabane struts in white) had a white swastika on the fuselage and a white top surface on the upper wing. Early style *Balkenkreuze* were marked on the wings and rudder.

31

Fokker Dr I 504/17 of Ltn Rudolf Rienau, *Jasta* 19, Balatre, April 1918

Rienau's Dr I (Wk-Nr 2131) carried the yellow and black tail markings of the *Jasta*, as well as a white cowling. His own insignia consisted of white candy stripes wrapped around the fuselage from the nose to the tailplane's leading edge.

32

Fokker Dr I 503/17 of Ltn Hans Körner, *Jasta* 19, Balatre, circa April 1918

Bearing unit markings similar to other Triplanes of *Jasta* 19, Körner's Dr I (Wk-Nr 2130) was marked with a unique zig-zag lightning bolt running from the white cowling to just under the tailplane on the fuselage sides. A similar, but smaller, bolt ran along the top fuselage decking. Körner's Dr I was fitted with an Oigee telescopic sight mounted between the two guns, and also had a central chin-rest fitted between the weapons.

33

Fokker Dr I 503/17 of Ltn Arthur Rahn, *Jasta* 19, Balatre, April 1918

Rahn's 503/17 was marked with his personal white diamond band between two white bands motif, which was painted directly on the streaky Fokker factory finish. His Triplane (Wk-Nr 2058) bore the standard *Staffel* 19 markings, and had the serial number re-marked in small characters just above the vertical arm of the rudder cross. In addition, a black and white deputy leader's streamer trailed from the rudder.

34

Fokker Dr I 426/17 of Vzfw Otto Esswein, *Jasta* 26, Halluin-Ost, May 1918

This aircraft (Wk-Nr 2010) displayed the distinctive *Staffel* 26 markings of a black cowling and broad black/white bands on the entire fuselage and tail surfaces. Esswein's personal marking was a black 'E' on a white band just aft of the cockpit. This was repeated on the centre section of the top wing. Signs of the alterations of the national insignia to succeeding forms of *Balkenkreuz* were distinctly evident through the thin white paint on the fuselage and rudder, and the crosses on the wings displayed a thin white border which had been reduced from a previous thicker form. A tube for a flare pistol and a rack for cartridges appeared below the cockpit sill.

35

Fokker Dr I (serial unconfirmed) of Ltn Fritz Loerzer, *Jasta* 26, Erchin, circa April 1918

Staffelführer Loerzer flew this Dr I painted in full unit markings on the fuselage and tail. The leading third of the top wing uppersurface was also painted black, as was the centre section of the same wing – these markings helped distinguish the CO's aircraft. This Dr I also had black wheel covers.

36

Fokker Dr I 577/17 of Ltn Rudolf Klimke, *Jasta* 27, Halluin-Ost, May 1918

This unit's *Staffel* markings included a yellow cowling, struts, wheel covers and rear fuselage. In the case of Klimke's 577/17 (Wk-Nr 2247), the latter included the fuselage cross area, which was probably a darker yellow due to the solid olive beneath that had been used to convert the national insignia to *Balkenkreuz* form. A yellow anchor adorned the fuselage sides just aft of the cockpit, and a similar anchor was painted in black on the upper centre area of the tailplane.

37

Fokker Dr I 206/17(?) of Oblt Hermann Göring, *Jasta* 27, Halluin-Ost, circa May 1918

Although the serial number is unconfirmed, the illustration depicts the colours applied to the Triplanes Göring flew as leader of *Jasta* 27 in May-June. Unlike other aircraft in his *Staffel*, his machines featured white struts, wheel covers, cowling and tail section to distinguish the CO's machine within the unit. The remainder of his Dr Is featured factory camouflage and early-style *Balkenkreuze*.

38

Fokker Dr I 521/17 of Oblt Robert Greim, *Jasta* 34b, Foucaucourt, June 1918

Staffelführer Greim's Dr I (Wk-Nr 2198) was marked with the forward fuselage in the usual streaked olive fashion, and the fuselage aft of the cockpit in the unit colour of 'whitish-silver'. Greim's individual emblem consisted of two large red bands encircling the fuselage, here divided by a thin band of the unit colour – this was supplemented by a red cowling. The rudder was white, and the struts were probably solid olive, with fully-bordered *Balkenkreuze* on the wings and fuselage.

39

Fokker Dr I (serial unconfirmed) of Vzfw Johann Pütz, *Jasta* 34b, Foucaucourt, May 1918

Pütz' Triplane was identical to Greim's machine as seen in profile 38 in most aspects, except that the pilot's personal colour, applied to the cowling and two fuselage bands, was a deep green. This was an ex-JG I aircraft, and featured an original small-area starboard aileron. When photographed, the insignia on the undersides of the bottom wing were still in iron cross form, although the rest had been changed to *Balkenkreuze*.

40

Fokker Dr I 441/17 of Ltn Heinrich Bongartz, *Jasta* 36, Erchin, March 1918

Bongartz' Dr I (Wk-Nr 2066) was in standard streaked camouflage overall, with the customary light blue-grey undersurfaces and struts. *Staffel* 36's unit symbol was a deep medium blue engine cowling. In addition, many of its Dr Is were marked with a supplementary iron cross insignia on the upper horizontal tail surface to help ensure identification from behind. The circular access panel aft of the cowling and the auxiliary undercarriage struts were also characteristics of the unit's Dr Is.

SELECTED BIBLIOGRAPHY

Bodenschatz, K, *Jagd in Flanderns Himmel.* Munich, 1935
Carisella, P and Ryan, J, *Who Killed the Red Baron?* Wakefield, MA, 1969
Ferko, A E, *Richthofen.* Berkhamsted, Herts, 1995
Franks, N, Bailey, F and Guest, R, *Above the Lines.* London, 1993
Franks, N, Giblin, H, and McCreery, N, *Under the Guns of the Red Baron.* London, 1995
Franks, N, and Giblin, H, *Under the Guns of the German Aces.* London, 1997
Imrie, A, *The Fokker Triplane.* London, 1992
Imrie, A, *Osprey Airwar 17: German Fighter Units – June 1917-1918.* London, 1978
Imrie, A, *Pictorial History of the German Army Air Service.* London, 1971
Imrie, A, *Vintage Warbirds 16: German Air Aces of World War One.* Poole, 1987
Jones, J, *King of Air Fighters.* London, 1934
Kilduff, P, *Germany's First Air Force 1914-1918.* London, 1991
Kilduff, P, *The Red Baron Combat Wing: Jagdgeschwader Richthofen in Battle.* London, 1997

Kilduff, P, *Richthofen: Beyond the Legend of the Red Baron.* New York, 1993
Langsdorff, W (ed.), *Flieger am Feind.* Gütersloh, circa 1935
Lawson, S (ed.), '*Jasta* 7 Under "Köbes"', *Cross & Cockade International Journal* Vol 25 No 3, 1994
Lee, A G, *No Parachute.* New York, 1970
MacMillan, N, *Into the Blue.* London, 1929
Neumann, G (ed.), *In der Luft Unbesiegt.* Munich, 1923
O'Connor, N, *Aviation Awards of Imperial Germany in World War I and the Men Who Earned Them, Vols I to VI.* Princeton, NJ, 1988 to 1999
Revell, A, *High in the Empty Blue.* Mountain View, CA, 1995
Richthofen, M, *Der rote Kampfflieger.* Berlin, 1933; (English translation P Kilduff, *The Red Baron.* New York, 1969)
Tutschek, A, *Stürme und Luftsiege.* Berlin, 1918
Udet, E, *Kreuz wider Kokarde.* Munich, 1918
Udet, E, *Mein Fliegerleben.* Berlin, 1935; (English translation R Riehn, *Ace of the Iron Cross.* New York, 1970)
Wills, K (ed.), 'The War Letters of Hauptmann Ritter von Tutschek', Part 2, *Over the Front: The League of WW I Aero Historians* Vol 4 No 1, 1989

INDEX

References to illustrations are shown in **bold**. Plates are shown
with page and caption locators in brackets.

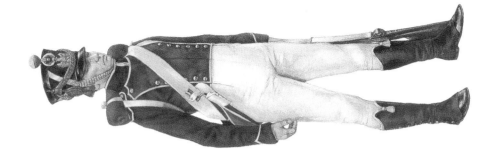 

FIND OUT MORE ABOUT OSPREY

❏ Please send me a FREE trial issue
   of Osprey Military Journal

❏ Please send me the latest listing of Osprey's publications

❏ I would like to subscribe to Osprey's e-mail newsletter

Title/rank _____

Name _____

Address _____

_____

_____

Postcode/zip _____ state/country _____

e-mail _____

Which book did this card come from?

_____

❏ I am interested in military history

My preferred period of military history is _____

❏ I am interested in military aviation

My preferred period of military aviation is _____

I am interested in *(please tick all that apply)*

❏ general history   ❏ militaria   ❏ model making
❏ wargaming   ❏ re-enactment

Please send to:

USA & Canada: Osprey Direct USA, c/o Motorbooks
International, P.O. Box 1, 729 Prospect Avenue, Osceola,
WI 54020

UK, Europe and rest of world:
Osprey Direct UK, P.O. Box 140, Wellingborough, Northants,
NN8 2FA, United Kingdom

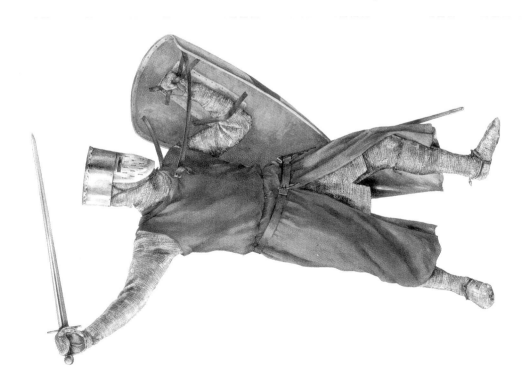

OSPREY
PUBLISHING

www.ospreypublishing.com

call our telephone hotline
for a free information pack

USA & Canada: 1-800-458-0454
UK, Europe and rest of world call:
+44 (0) 1933 443 863

Young Guardsman
Figure taken from *Warrior 22:
Imperial Guardsman 1799–1815*
Published by Osprey
Illustrated by Christa Hook

Knight, c.1190
Figure taken from *Warrior 1: Norman Knight 950 – 1204AD*
Published by Osprey
Illustrated by Christa Hook

POSTCARD